Adverse Childhood Experiences, Attachment, and the Early Years Learning Environment

Adverse Childhood Experiences, Attachment, and the Early Years Learning Environment explores the concept of learning by presenting research and illustrations from practice on three major topics: adverse childhood experiences, attachment, and environment. Each child has a unique reaction to adversity in the early years, and the book discusses the effect upon approach and avoidance motivation for learning, and the rationale of trauma-informed practice. The influence from a secure attachment figure is explored, and links between emotions and involvement are presented.

The book highlights the current indoor and outdoor use of natural green spaces as a response to attention-fatigue and promotes comprehension of the issues in a context of attention restoration theory. Intervention for extended families is presented as an approach to supporting development and attainment in each generation, and to achieving a legacy beyond the professional network.

This book will appeal to academics, researchers, and postgraduate students in the fields of early years care and education. It will also appeal to those working within children's services.

Hazel G. Whitters is a Senior Early Years Worker/Child Protection Officer in a family service in Glasgow, Scotland. Hazel's research includes studies on the parent–professional relationship in child protection, and attachment in the early years, and primary 1–3.

Adverse Childhood Experiences, Attachment, and the Early Years Learning Environment

Research and Inclusive Practice

Hazel G. Whitters

LONDON AND NEW YORK

First published 2020 by Routledge

2 Park Square, Milton Park, Abingdon, Oxon OX14 4RN

605 Third Avenue, New York, NY 10017

Routledge is an imprint of the Taylor & Francis Group, an informa business

First issued in paperback 2021

Copyright © 2020 Hazel G. Whitters

The right of Hazel G. Whitters to be identified as author of this work has been asserted by her in accordance with sections 77 and 78 of the Copyright, Designs and Patents Act 1988.

All rights reserved. No part of this book may be reprinted or reproduced or utilised in any form or by any electronic, mechanical, or other means, now known or hereafter invented, including photocopying and recording, or in any information storage or retrieval system, without permission in writing from the publishers.

Notice:
Product or corporate names may be trademarks or registered trademarks, and are used only for identification and explanation without intent to infringe.

Publisher's Note

The publisher has gone to great lengths to ensure the quality of this reprint but points out that some imperfections in the original copies may be apparent.

British Library Cataloguing-in-Publication Data
A catalogue record for this book is available from the British Library

Library of Congress Cataloging-in-Publication Data
A catalog record has been requested for this book

ISBN: 978-0-367-90196-7 (hbk)
ISBN: 978-1-03-217575-1 (pbk)
DOI: 10.4324/9781003022985

Typeset in Times New Roman
by Deanta Global Publishing Services, Chennai, India

I dedicate this book to early years researchers and practitioners throughout the world. Your motivation, enthusiasm, expertise, and commitment to working with children are invaluable, and much valued in guiding the next generation to be successful, happy contributors, and responsible citizens. I include a dedication to my husband, John, whose continuous support and encouragement has enabled me to achieve. Thank you.

Contents

	Introduction	1
1	Adverse childhood experiences	6
2	Attachment	27
3	Learning environments in the earliest years	48
4	Adverse childhood experiences, attachment, and the early years learning environment	72
	Index	83

Introduction

Abstract

The first 1,000 days of a child's life are a significant period for learning. Multiple complex and inter-dependent processes occur which are influenced by epigenetics, emotional wellbeing, and availability of opportunities. This book explores the concept of learning by presenting research and illustrations from practice on three major topics: adverse childhood experiences, attachment, and environment. Each child has a unique interpretation, and reaction to, adversity in the earliest years, and Chapter 1 discusses the effect upon approach and avoidance motivation for learning, and the rationale of trauma-informed practice. The influence from a secure attachment figure is explored in Chapter 2, and links are presented between emotions and involvement. The third chapter highlights the current indoor and outdoor use of natural green spaces as a response to attention-fatigue, and promotes comprehension of the issues in a context of attention restoration theory. The book concludes by focusing upon further influences on learning from the child's patterns of play in the form of schemas, and discusses the challenges of quality assurance. Intervention for extended families is presented as an approach to supporting development and attainment in each generation, and to achieving a legacy beyond the professional network.

Background information

This book commenced with a plan to explore learning environments in the home and services in the context of a child's earliest years. After a few months of research, I realised that I could not separate a study on environment from the catalyst which is intrinsically linked to human development – the attachment relationship. Additionally, I could not present information on an optimum learning environment without reflecting on the significance of each child's interpretation, and involvement with her world, which takes into account stress responses. In order to promote understanding on adversity a reader requires information on normative reactions from children within the same context. The manuscript plan was subsequently reviewed and re-configured to encompass three concepts: adverse childhood experiences, attachment, and learning environments.

There are multiple textbooks on attachment, numerous national and international research briefs on childhood adversities, and curricular guidance on the creation of positive learning environments; however, many writers have separated these three concepts. This book promotes the complementariness of, and inextricable links between, the three aspects in a context of learning in the early years.

No composite universal approach can be created which responds effectively to education and care of children within every playroom or classroom, in diverse communities and countries throughout our world. Generic strategies for guidance often bypass the impact of cultural influence in organisations, and fail to capture the importance of utilising positive endemic features within a locality. The book does not present an optimum environment for learning in the earliest years but publicises the importance of acknowledging and responding to adversity, creating rich and personalised circumstances for brain development, and maintaining secure attachment with a primary/secondary carer in services, and at home. I am passionate about empowering professionals to use their personalities, and vocational skills, to compliment practice guidance, and to be upskilled and inspired by an increase in comprehension.

Chapter 1: adverse childhood experiences

Knowledge of adversities can be sourced from a variety of disciplines, for example, social science, neuroscience, health, education, social work, public policy, and early childhood. This chapter refers to research examples from each of these fields to promote a deeper understanding of the phenomena, and to promote discussion on the rationale for current policies. Learning, and comprehending a sense of self, requires exposure to opportunities and internal motivation to accumulate knowledge from diverse and predictable experiences. Positive and negative interactions with the world shape our interpretation, reactions, and actions. Over time neural connections are formed and consolidated, and the inner working model is changed. Research indicates that the earliest experiences have a major influence upon these processes, and implicit memories are retained due to the context of emotional reaction.

The original research which presented a link between specific adversities, as experienced in the earliest years, and negative physical, mental, and emotional consequences in later life, was conducted in the United States and published in 1998 (Felitti et al., 1998). Findings from this longitudinal research have been used to influence the United States' policies, and to create positive responses to the issues from strategic and operational perspectives (Children's Bureau, 2018).

In 2017 a decision was made by the four United Kingdom nations to identify strategic and practical responses to the issues of child poverty, low attainment, poor health throughout the life-span, and strife within communities (Smith, 2018). During the last two years findings from the research of Felitti et al. (1998) have been catapulted to the forefront of practice. Numerous health, education, and social work professionals have undergone training, and several large conferences on this topic have been held throughout the United Kingdom. The concept of trauma-informed practice has emerged, and Chapter 1 contributes to this debate.

Practice examples from early years environments are presented to support an understanding of theory in practice. Services are bound by policy and led by curriculum as applicable to each country; however, the Eco-Schools programme encompasses countries from throughout the world, and this is highlighted as an international response to adversities. Epigenetics has come to the fore of research and practice in the field, and provides insight into the concepts of approach and avoidance motivation in the learning context. The chapter highlights current use of different mediums to share knowledge and promote change in the skills of primary carers, for example video feedback and shared play sessions, as responses to the diverse needs of parents.

Chapter 2: attachment

The second aspect for consideration is human relationships which is the focus of Chapter 2. Many years have passed since James Robertson and John Bowlby conducted research on relationship-based practice within a 1950s hospital setting, and introduced the concept of secure attachment to human development (Page, 2016). The legacy of these theorists continues to impact significantly upon childcare and education in the 21st century.

The chapter describes the rationale of attachment theory, and the creation of a positive relationship within a nurturing environment. Practice examples from the early years setting, for example the promotion of positive behaviour, are described in the context of the secure relationship between key worker–child, and parent–child, in a nursery setting. The profound effects from complex trauma upon learning are reviewed alongside toxic stress, affect regulation, and dissociation.

Expectations of practitioners in the early years sector have escalated in the last 20 years. The early years worker has a multitude of responsibilities: to teach, to care, and to protect; to observe, to assess, and to evaluate; to participate, to scaffold, and to communicate; and to integrate, to include, and to play with our youngest citizens during formative years. Attachment is associated with good mental health, and provides a developmental foundation for increasing resilience throughout the lifespan; however, challenges to the practitioner are discussed in the context of relationship-based practice with children who have negative relational experiences.

Chapter 3: learning environments

Chapter 3 presents illustrative examples from the early years context to demonstrate the learning space as internal and external to the child. The chapter introduces the topic with our first learning environment, pre-birth in the womb, and describes inter-generational and epigenetic influences from the mother and extended family.

Childhoods of the 21st century take place within two predominant environments – home and services. The concept of home is examined as multiple "home" environments for children are common due to a variety of circumstances which encompass daily family life. For example many parents are estranged, and consequently shared-care arrangements emerge for the children: some children have temporary homes within short-term respite care, or longer-term foster-care. Many families have access to support from relatives, kinship carers, or others, and informal arrangements result in periods of childhood out-with the birth-family home. Emotional and physical transitions are explored in theory, and the significance to learning is illustrated through practice examples.

Services present education in child-centred and child-led environments, for example early years settings, schools and associated leisure, and after-school care. Currently services in the United Kingdom, United States, and elsewhere receive specific funding for interventions which support good mental health of children, and impact positively upon the attainment gap. There is a particular focus upon accessing outdoor environments as practical responses to these issues. Concerns for parents, for example, choice of setting, are explored through research, in addition to the impact of physical structure and layout of a service upon a child's ability and capacity to learn and develop.

Outcomes from play in green spaces are presented which include an increase in environmental sensitivity, and a discussion of hard and soft fascination. Attention restoration theory is used to gain understanding of the influence of experiences outdoors and pictorial representations of the natural world. Links are discussed between characteristics of attention deficit hyperactivity disorder, and general attention-fatigue, through research and practice examples. A description of green walls presents the current approach of architects in representing the natural experience indoors.

Introduction 5

The reader is given an opportunity to reflect upon transitions, and the impact on resilience, and coping strategies which are acquired within a relationship of secure attachment. Resilience liberates the child to recognise and to embrace learning in different contexts. Ultimately an increase in motivation will activate the child's readiness to learn, and his ability to be an active agent in seeking out, and capitalising upon, opportunities. These examples highlight the plasticity of the human brain, and the ability for adaptation and achievement in diverse circumstances.

Chapter 4: adverse childhood experiences, attachment, and the early years learning environment.

The final chapter reviews the complementariness of the three concepts in a context of learning, and the expected outcomes of intentional or adaptive learners. The role of educator is discussed in addition to the involvement and wellbeing of each learner. The impact from locality is described in the context of early childhood, as is the occurrence of a community of practice within a service and environs. This chapter presents theory and practice of inclusive pedagogy, and reflects upon diversity, schemas, and the child's expression of knowledge in different modalities.

My experience in research and practice has shown that the impact of findings can be diminished, and the emphasis changed by presentation of information. Undue pressure can be imposed upon the early years workforce by the use of teaching exemplars which portray best practice strategies. The chapter presents accountability, assessment, and cultural awareness as significant factors to consider in establishing an effective early years learning environment.

References

Children's Bureau. 2018, 'Adverse childhood experiences', viewed 26 December, 2018, https://childwelfare.gov/topics/preventing/preventionmonth/resources/ace/.

Felitti, V.J., Anda, R.F., Nordenberg, D., Williamson, D.F., Spitz, A.M., Edwards, V., Koss, M.P. & Marks, J.S. 1998, 'Relationships of childhood abuse and household dysfunction to many of the leading causes of death in adults', *American Journal of Preventive Medicine*, vol. 14, no. 4. viewed 25 December, 2017, https://nhs.scot.knowledge.network

Page, J. 2016, 'The Legacy of John Bowlby's attachment theory', in T. David, K. Goouch & S. Powell (eds.), *The Routledge international handbook of philosophies and theories of early childhood education and care*, Routledge, New York, pp. 80–90.

Smith, L. 2018, *Adverse childhood experiences (ACEs): educational interventions*, The Institute for Research and Innovation in Social Services (Iriss), Glasgow.

1 Adverse childhood experiences

This chapter discusses adverse childhood experiences (ACEs) in a context of research, policy, and practice. A deficit model is explored, as is the creation of practical approaches for interventions in the child's earliest years.

Example from practice

The train swayed from side to side on exiting the station. Cold horizontal rain and pellets of spring hail buffeted against the windows of the carriages – a noisy backdrop for the Monday morning commuters as they balanced with bowed heads, phone-checking and sending texts rapidly. Does the modern day mobile phone promote secure attachment between two people? Is this the medium we use to maintain our circle of security and to explore our world from a platform of information and reciprocal relationships?

We stood together in the aisles of this train – student, lawyer, lecturer, computer analyst, parent, politician, and more. A scene replicated many times in many cities. Tolerable stresses invaded the lives of these carriage neighbours. Will the train be late? Will the taxi-rank be full? Will the electronic barrier be working? What to do with a wet umbrella? How to check confidential emails in a busy carriage?

I quietly considered these issues as the train traversed from Glasgow to Edinburgh, and I gained realisation that daily tolerable stresses often relate to potential adversities – if this... then that... The stress is self-imposed as we attempt to prepare for eventualities. As humans, we seek consistency and predictability in our lives. We function best with a pre-conceived plan, and several caveats as required. We are confident in accepting different pathways in our everyday lives if we are embraced by resilience, but what if the "tolerable" stress is an unwelcome addition upon minds and bodies already affected by historical adversities? These consequential effects may be latent but ready to emerge, and incited by daily influences.

I alighted into the dry cold of Edinburgh station, and my focus sharpened as I sought a taxi. I rejected the long snaking queue of commuters, changed plan, and walked quickly towards my destination. I was attending a Child Protection conference. A time for professionals to meet, to discuss, to agree and disagree on a topic which is current to childcare and education today: adverse childhood experiences. I hunched my shoulders against the biting wind, quickened pace, and activated my resilience in response to this Monday morning stress.

Adverse childhood experiences

Research

Twenty-one years ago researchers published findings from a longitudinal study on human development (Felitti et al., 1998). This study featured participants from the United States, and investigated childhood adversities as potential negative influences upon development, with a particular emphasis on obesity. Felitti et al. (1998) identified ten adverse childhood experiences: physical, verbal, and sexual abuse; physical and emotional neglect; and mental illness, incarcerated relative, domestic violence, parental separation, and substance abuse. These aspects are commonly grouped, and recognised throughout the world, within the three categories of *abuse, neglect*, and *household* adversities. During the intervening years, the research on this topic has been broadened to include current adversities, for example, domestic violence between adolescents, community violence, and homelessness (Bellazaire, 2018).

Smith (2018) commented that references to adversities in childhood have increased tenfold since 2010 in publications throughout the world. This author conducted an extensive literature review on the topic, and identified a lack of longitudinal evidence on generic strategies. The report did indicate a wealth of knowledge gained from evaluation of specific interventions within particular areas and circumstances.

The latest literature review was published this year by Di Lemma et al. (2019). One hundred interventions, as responses to childhood adversities, were investigated and four common themes emerged: parental support, relationship-based practice and increasing resilience, early intervention in response to identified adversities, and finally using strategies to support trauma in relation to specific adversities. This report placed particular emphasis on the use of universal and targeted intervention in an inter-generational context of primary carers and children. Acknowledgement was made to the long-lasting impact of childhood adversities, and the significance of taking a holistic approach to intervention within families.

8 *Adverse childhood experiences*

Poverty

The United States have referred to the findings of Felitti et al. (1998) in policy and practice, and the increase in knowledge and understanding has informed legislation. To date, from January to May 2018, there were 68 proposals in 25 states which incorporated adverse childhood experiences and trauma-informed practices (Bellazaire, 2018). The effect of poverty is recognised as the most common adverse childhood experience in every American state, and in 2018, 25% of children in the United States lived below federal poverty level.

Research uses theory to explore the concept of poverty and the far-reaching effects upon a family unit which encompass physical and mental health, executive functioning, and attainment. Living in poverty can eliminate or reduce opportunities to reflect, and to plan ahead. It can remove the reassurance of predictability, positive anticipation, and the emotions which are experienced by the majority of the population of parents as they create a fulfilling lifestyle for their children and themselves. The toxic stress which accompanies poverty can cause a family to operate in crisis mode, and negativity can be transferred to many different aspects of family life, including relationships. The research by Shonkoff and Fisher (2013) recommends that increasing executive functioning of adult carers should be a primary focus of intervention, alongside practical responses to poverty. These authors emphasise the plasticity of the human brain throughout the life-span – baby to child to adult. For practitioners this delivers an important message of hope, and identifies a route to change which encompasses different generations of families, and creates a legacy beyond the professional network.

Other countries have applied comprehension of the findings on adversities to policy. The Scottish Government (2018) used the findings in the National Practice Model termed *Getting It Right for Every Child* as examples of issues which should be considered in a care plan for each child. A national plan aims to reduce the number of children who live in poverty to less than 10% by 2030 (Royal College of Paediatrics and Child Health, 2019). Bellis et al. (2014) reported that Europe has committed to promoting a life course approach to good health by inter-disciplinary interventions.

Example from practice

The holistic view of development, and intervention, has been embraced by many countries throughout the world who implement the Eco-Schools programme (Foundation for Environmental Education, 2015). It is promoted as the largest sustainable school programme in the world, incorporating 67 countries on five continents and creating a universal link through knowledge and understanding for 19.5 million children. In 2015 the United Nations identified 17 goals to sustain our world, and these outcomes have been adopted throughout the Eco-Schools programme and provide a framework for services to promote ways to protect our planet, and our citizens.

Sustainable Development Goals (Foundation for Environmental Education, 2015):

1 *No poverty.*
2 *Zero hunger.*
3 *Good health and wellbeing.*
4 *Quality education.*
5 *Gender equality.*
6 *Clean water and sanitation.*
7 *Affordable and clean energy.*
8 *Decent work and economic growth.*
9 *Industry, innovation, and infrastructure.*
10 *Reduced inequalities.*
11 *Sustainable cities and communities.*
12 *Responsible consumption and production.*
13 *Climate action.*
14 *Life below water.*
15 *Life on land.*
16 *Peace and justice strong institutions.*
17 *Partnership for goals.*

Tackling poverty and protecting the planet are key aspects to the rationale, and the Eco-Schools programme's projects are prime examples of educational intervention which is applied in response to a cultural context of each community, and which accesses the knowledge and skills from young and old.

Mental health

Links have also been made to mental health issues. It is known that one third of mental health disorders in the world can be associated with adverse childhood experiences (McLaughlin, 2017). In 2017 figures were published which estimated that 800,000 children in England have a mental health problem. The National Institute for Health and Care Excellence(NICE) in 2017 termed families and communities as protective factors which support resilience in individuals and wider society. The Scottish Government has included this approach within the Scottish Mental Health Strategy 2017–2027 (Scottish Government, 2017).

Trauma-informed practice

The study by Felitti et al. (1998) focused upon the deficit model, and this presentation of information has been a common criticism of the investigation; however, research findings rarely change practice directly but instead provide rich foundations of knowledge which prompt discussion, and support comprehension and development of practice. There was no causal link established but findings indicated a "graded relationship" between accumulation of adversities, the period in which influences were experienced, and risk factors associated with death in adulthood. These are complex issues which need to be studied as separate concepts in their contexts, and the links between aspects and multifarious effects need also to be considered.

In 2014 Larkin, and two colleagues who participated in the aforementioned research, identified cognition as important to an individual's perception, interpretation, and reaction to circumstances as positive or negative (Larkin et al., 2014). This research also made reference to the emergence of stress when an individual feels unable to respond to the demands of a situation. The report indicates that resilience is actioned by a person changing the source of stress *or* changing his emotional reaction to the stress. The context is challenging for researchers and practitioners, and there is great complexity in understanding the inter-play of internal and external influences upon each person; however, awareness of these difficulties has resulted in the current approach of trauma-informed practice which necessarily considers the individual's perspective.

It is important that strategic and practical responses to childhood adversities capitalise upon existing approaches within the fields of health and education. The World Health Organisation emphasises the significance of services taking a holistic view of childhood influences, and recommends that responses should traverse different work sectors, for example, justice, welfare, commercial, and civil society. This report is a mid-plan publication in the context of the European Child Maltreatment Prevention Action Plan 2015–2020. It publicises the current context of 55 million children in the World Health Organisation European region who suffer from maltreatment (Sethi et al., 2018).

An example of this issue is illustrated in the study conducted by Bright et al. (2014), in the United States, which investigated potential links between adversities in childhood and tooth condition as presence of caries. The findings indicated a cumulative effect from the number of adversities and the extent of tooth decay in childhood (Bright et al., 2014). This research focus suggests that the need for intervention could be identified within dental health programmes which are already disseminated throughout populations. A second example is gained from Cardoso and his colleagues who published research in 2018 from a large study of almost 1,000 participants. The study investigated links between childhood trauma and sleep disturbances in adulthood. The findings recommended that historical trauma should be investigated during assessment and intervention for adult sleep issues (Cardoso et al., 2018). These two examples of research indicate that population health interventions could be utilised, and potentially developed, by considering the issue of childhood adversities.

Epigenetics

Epigenetics is another field which contributes to this debate. A study was published in 2018 which indicated links between epigenetic changes and early childhood trauma. This research, by Bearer and Mulligan (2018), used saliva and blood samples to explore differences in the immune system, as well as hormone regulation in adults who had experienced historical adversities versus a norm group. The findings contribute to identifying diagnostic markers, and it may be that this approach could be incorporated into an already-existing screening programme.

Countries continue to imply a causal link in publications: for example, in 2019 the United Kingdom's Government issued a briefing paper which clearly linked four or more adverse childhood experiences with a suicide risk of 30 times greater than the norm (House of Commons, 2019). The term "ACE scoring" is being applied within publications, but this generalisation does not reflect the frequency or severity of adversities, or existence of protective factors, or any links to an individual's reaction. The knowledge is informative, emotive, and demands attention from the public and policymakers but understanding of the issues must also be sought. Removing the source of adversity does not equate to minimising or erasing the effect of the adverse experience in childhood or adulthood.

A descriptive language has evolved as findings are applied to practice; for example, household adversities, family and community protective factors, personal vulnerability, acquired resilience, and trauma-informed practice. These descriptions can be sourced directly to practitioners, and demonstrate a bridging of the gap between academic presentation of information and terminology as applicable to the field. Last year the American Government publicised that adverse childhood experiences were "traumatic events" which occurred prior to the age of 18 (Children's Bureau, 2018).

The term "post-traumatic stress disorder" (PTSD) has become synonymous with adversities in daily life. Devaney and Duffy (2017) identified symptoms of PTSD as encompassing memories of the event in different formats, for example, flashbacks during waking hours, nightmares during sleep, re-enactment during play; I feel that the most significant aspect for intervention is the change to a child's interpretation and the reaction to her world.

These authors commented that this disorder can become chronic, and I have recently noted that the acronym PTSD can be seen on nursery referral information from health professionals with reference to childbirth. In my work of over 30 years I have not been aware of the actual birthing process being highlighted as a source of long-term trauma. Commonly a parent's inability to cope with daily needs and behaviour of a child is the inter-disciplinary referral rationale for placement in early years services. It is interesting that this focus upon adversities has resulted in health professionals considering childbirth as a primary source of trauma for parent and child with long-term effects.

Neuroscience

Evidence from neuroscience has rapidly entered training for practitioners, and has been depicted as a valid source for understanding the effect of trauma upon development. Classic publications such as *Early Intervention: the Next Steps* by Graham Allen (2011) showed the dramatic effect of stimulation and non-stimulation on the brain through adjoining brain-scans on the front cover of the research report. These photographs of the small brain and the large brain, published in 2011, created intense focus upon the field of neuroscience in the United Kingdom, and the topic has been introduced to undergraduate training courses in childcare and education. This symbolism is a valuable tool which can be used to activate an interest in a particular topic, and attract academics and practitioners seeking out further learning.

Edwards (2018) gives evidence of brain plasticity in the form of synaptic remodelling although this research does not identify the actual processes by which environmental stress affects brain growth. The report indicates that neural changes in a context of child abuse are similar, and potentially undistinguishable from changes in a context of psychiatric disorders; however, neuroscience has supported strategic and practical decision-making by indicating the critical period for change in brain structure, and providing evidence of positive effects from the development of parenting skills and increased opportunities for children.

Approach and avoidance motivation

It was with anticipation that I accessed the latest working paper from the National Scientific Council on the Developing Child (2018) on the concept of motivation. Motivation to learn is closely associated with executive functioning and attainment throughout the life-span, and it is important to understand the factors or circumstances which facilitate or hinder learning processes (Whitters, 2019).

Research in the field of neuroscience provides details of internal changes within the brain which are observed externally as behaviour, actions, and emotions. The inner working model (Bowlby, 1979) retains knowledge and personal interpretation of every experience, and the associated implicit memories. These unique memories can be activated by explicit features, which are external to the individual, for example, an environmental prompt.

Harvard University researchers have described the impact of chemical signals in the brain as the creation of links between memory, emotions, and an experience. Chemicals include dopamine, serotonin, norepinephrine, glutamate, and opioids which occur naturally. The result is the formation of expectations by an individual, and actions to achieve a goal. The research distinguishes between two types of motivation: **approach motivation** and **avoidance motivation** (National Scientific Council on the Developing Child, 2018).

Approach motivation is a facilitating factor which leads to actions for the purpose of fulfilling a recognisable goal. *Avoidance motivation* directs an individual away from a potential threat (National Scientific Council on the Developing Child, 2018). Both types of motivation are based upon the release of chemicals and a chain of neural processes as previously described. The majority of the population develop a balance of approach and avoidance motivation which commences in childhood but some individuals may demonstrate a tendency to excessive reward-seeking or danger-avoidance. These behaviours are associated with attention-deficit/hyperactivity, depression, substance abuse, anxiety, and post-traumatic stress. It is known that a secure attachment relationship can impact positively on an over-activated amygdala which recognises many daily experiences as threatening, and without reward.

One driver of approach motivation is the human being's inherent instinct to learn. The child or adult will anticipate the outcome of an experience in the context of a familiar or anticipated reward. An attachment figure, for example a teacher or parent, can support a child in interpreting a forthcoming experience as positive. This positivity results in a chemical surge in the brain of dopamine which increases links between emotion and memory; therefore implicit memories of the same or similar experience can be recalled, and contribute to approach motivation on subsequent occasions. Alternatively, lack of positivity from a primary carer can result in a child acquiring learned helplessness (Day et al., 2017).

I believe that the issue of "learned helplessness" can be interpreted from three perspectives, which require different interventions:

- A parent may not actively support achievement in a child, and indirectly undermine potential for development of resilience, and pride in attainment.
- A parent may directly abuse a child emotionally, physically, or through neglect, which adversely affects the child's understanding of himself as an active agent.
- A parent may demonstrate inability and incapacity to cope effectively with daily living which is subsequently emulated by a child. For example, domestic violence presents many different adversities in a household and can result in the victim, whether mother or father, having low self-esteem and an immature sense of self.

Example from practice

Paulina and her three-year-old daughter were spending time in their local nursery play-room. It was the induction period for Florentina who was actively demonstrating a "flight" response to this unknown experience. The new nursery girl was copying the behaviour and intentions portrayed by her mother.

Paulina's purple waterproof jacket was firmly zipped, and she wore a little black hand-bag positioned diagonally across her body. Cues of exiting quickly were being shared explicitly with her daughter through body language and actions. Paulina folded her arms, refused the offer of a seat, and stood near the door. In one hand this young mother held a mobile phone which had a furry pink cover. Paulina moved her phone back and forth as if seeking a response.

The use of mobile phones has become embedded in the daily imaginative play scenarios of our youngest children. Similar patterns of play are repeated by children throughout early years settings, and mobile phones have particular associations for each child which relates to family cultural habits, and community lifestyles.

It is interesting to observe a child copying the actions of an adult as he or she talks, argues, laughs, listens, and agrees to an imaginary plan – a downward swipe on the pretend phone, the conversation ends, and the child walks briskly forward as he or she puts the agreed-upon plan into action which invariably involves leaving an imaginary house.

The key worker hovered near Florentina and her mother, and I could see that this staff member was anxious in case the phone policy had to be actioned. "No mobile phone usage in services" is a welcome mandate from data protection acts around the world, but it is challenging to implement effectively, and diplomatically, in the early stages of a professional–parent relationship. When entering unfamiliar situations, for example an early years service, parents use their phones as transition objects, as representation of attachment figures, as a prompt and prior commitment to escape from the situation, or as a comfort object. Paulina held her pink mobile phone, and Florentina clutched a brown baby teddy-bear.

Settling into nursery is difficult for parents and children. Over time every practitioner gains a wealth of experience in identifying strategies relating to distraction, comfort, reassurance, and promotion of fun. We all have intimate knowledge of, and personal preferences for, the "best" toys for settling children – the surprise of bubbles being blown, the unexpected distraction of a jack-in-the-box, the quick return from a simple shape-sorter, a ball rolling slowly into the play-room venue, the attraction of tiny hand-held toys, and the use of transition objects. The child's own toy can transpose the memory of home into a different environment, and create an instant reminder of an attachment figure.

Florentina's face crumpled, and she looked anxiously from her mother to the door as her eyes pleaded for escape. The little girl was oblivious to the Aladdin's cave of toys in the nursery, and I quickly detected that the key to settling our new learner was settling her primary carer, Paulina.

The driver of avoidance motivation is survival. The child will associate an experience with the emotion of fear or revulsion. This negativity results in a chemical surge in the brain of stress hormones such as norepinephrine. In practice, the terms *fight*, *flight*, or *freeze* are used to describe the child's reaction to perceived negative influences. During this period a chain of processes occurs to prepare the body for action. One process is dependent on another, and include a faster heart-rate, rise of blood glucose level, and an increase in oxygen to the brain. This overall body response mechanism ensures the safety of the child; however, his or her reaction may not be commensurate with the context. Children who have experienced adversity, particularly in early childhood, may demonstrate a major reaction to a minor circumstance. The earliest experiences create a blue-print for interpretation, reaction, and action. Children's behaviour may be termed aggressive, and impulsive, as a result of their extreme reactions to daily adversities which would generally be regarded as tolerable stresses.

Resilience

Research into adverse childhood experiences has continued steadily throughout the world since 1998. During my early childhood, in the 1970s, parents were their children's ambassadors who would promote a good health mantra in the form of a balanced diet, adequate sleep for brain development, and regular exercise outdoors. Childhoods of the 21st century are supported by parents *and* services such as nursery, school, and after-school care, in a context of policies and procedures. Evidence-based practice strategies and current research promote the same three features as positive responses to childhood adversities (National Council on the Developing Child, 2016). I feel it is essential that previous knowledge is not discarded regardless of whether the source is validated formal research or informal anecdotal life skills from family. Learning by professionals and parents must encompass guidance from research as well as values, attitudes, and approaches which have been identified, tried, and honed within a local culture over many years.

Resilience is a multi-faceted concept which parents and professionals recognise as necessary to operate effectively in the microsystem of daily living, in addition to managing the long-term effects of negative childhood experiences. Reaction and ultimately resilience to adversity is personal, and unique to each one of us. Research identifies that this human attribute is influenced by personality, internal predisposition which is genetically based, and experiences external to the child (National Council on the Developing Child, 2011). The individuality of resilience is a common topic among practitioners in the fields of early years and education. Many services create transitions between nursery and primary school, and collegiate discussions often focus upon the different reactions of younger and older siblings to the same household adversity.

It is interesting and unusual that *parental resilience* is highlighted as a protective factor in the aforementioned report by the World Health Organisation (Sethi et al., 2018). This issue was also reported by Perry (2014) who recommended that the treatment for primary carers and for their children who have experienced the same or similar trauma should be complimentary. In 2018, the National Council on Children, Families and Relationships submitted a policy brief to the American Government which recommended two-generation intervention programmes to empower local communities, and strengthen parent–child relationships. The brief categorised these strategic and operational approaches as direct responses to adverse childhood experiences (Palm & Cooke, 2018). Many studies identify the inter-generational effect of adversities, along with the complexity of risk, protective factors, and personal vulnerability, as contributory to negative impact (Shonkoff & Fisher, 2013).

A primary carer leads a child in his or her interpretation of the world which may be positive and support the development of resilience to tolerable stress, or which can induce negativity and incite fear and anxiety. Adult carers who have experienced abuse in childhood may continue to demonstrate reactions and behaviours acquired as an infant which minimise potential for threat, but also restrict learning. This presentation of fear is rapidly adopted by a young child.

Research indicates that approach and avoidance motivation are formed prior to language development, and these attributes can be observed in young babies (National Scientific Council on the Developing Child, 2018). Motivation is driven by internal and external influences, which may be regarded as intrinsic drivers within the child, and extrinsic feedback from an external source. It is known that external rewards, for example material prizes or excessive praise, can undermine the positive effect from intrinsic drivers (Whitters, 2018). Children may develop dependency on a reward system and their approach to motivation, over time, can encompass an expectation of external feedback.

These processes can diminish the development of resilience, and result in the child's need for direction and recognition from others. In practice, a child may appear to be "pleasing" the peer or adult who provides this reward by following and pre-empting the other person's ideas in the learning context. The child's sense of self is immature which affects executive functioning and attainment. These circumstances ultimately inhibit development by impacting negatively upon approach motivation. Ideally a balance of intrinsic drivers and extrinsic feedback which reflects the child's achievements by an attachment figure are effective supports in the learning process.

Childhood and adolescent years are times when humans demonstrate increased neural responses to social integration, desire for inclusion in a chosen peer group, or rejection. Children who have experienced abusive situations will be particularly attuned and sensitive to the reactions of others in this context. External feedback supports the young person's understanding of him or herself, and representation in family and social networks. Extrinsic return can promote integration by educating the child about lifestyle expectations of birth-family, religion, or peer or societal culture.

Young children and adolescents may present an increase in risk-taking and attention-seeking behaviours as they crave social and cultural feedback from their microsystem of contacts, and try to establish a framework for living. The old adage in the early years sector of "ignoring negative behaviour" has to be interpreted in this new understanding which we have gained from neuroscience. Comprehending behaviour and actions as the child's or adolescent's communication strategies informs responsive parenting, and professional practice. It can be relatively easy for adults to accept that a young two-year-old's tantrum is a request for secure attachment, and social boundaries with which to make sense of her world; however, it may be more challenging to gain the same interpretation of erratic and dangerous teenage behaviours.

Researchers, practitioners, and policy-makers have a responsibility to pool their knowledge and understanding, and to share this information with parents and one another. I have always found that parents are keen to gain an explanation of their children's behaviours which provides a foundation for change in parent and child. It is often the case that parents are reminded of personal circumstances which were experienced during their own childhood years. Witnessing the dawning of realisation when a parent gains comprehension of her own historical adversities, emotions, fears, and behaviour is a striking moment for the service-provider in addition to the service-user.

Early intervention

A significant approach to practice which has emerged in the last decade focuses upon recognising achievement in the processes of an activity rather than solely praising an outcome. The practical implication is an increase in resilience to adversity. Describing the processes to a child verbally can contribute to a transferrable skill base, and enable coping strategies to be transposed to other circumstances, with or without the presence of adult carer. It is essential that an adult exhibits belief in what each child that he or she can achieve. This supportive relationship influences approach motivation, and facilitates learning particularly in a new context.

Example from practice

Video interactive guidance (VIG) is a relatively new approach to the development of parenting skills. Research indicates a link between the formal use of this tool, and an increase in attachment between parent and child (Landor et al., 2010). This modern medium of communication by use of video feedback can also be applied in an informal capacity within services. Today's generation of parents are conversant with videos as a communication device to share children's achievements through the use of mobile phones.

Over many years of working with vulnerable families I have learned to seek out opportunities to share skills with parents informally, and within the contexts of formally implemented parenting programmes. I have learned to capitalise upon a parent's interest which may be known to services or shared spontaneously. I have learned to accept a parent's overture quickly, regardless of whether my plan has to change. My outcome is to engage the primary carer to focus upon care and education of child and self, and to activate latent parenting skills, in addition to new learning.

Nee arrived early for an interactive session with myself and her two-year-old son, Song-Song. As I knelt on the pale green rug, chosen for its aesthetic values, I heard a timid knock on the play-room door which had been propped open with the ubiquitous nursery door-stop – a pencil. Nee smiled as she stepped over the door-stop, and offered to help me to tidy up. In actual fact I was setting the scene for her parent–child play session. An ideal opportunity had emerged!

The young mother and I bowed our heads together as we crouched down in this little room, and looked into the big red box of artefacts. I asked Nee to choose **her** favourite toys, and together we discussed each play prompt by linking the items to Nee's knowledge and to Song-Song's needs, and with gentle encouragement the mother positioned each toy carefully upon the green rug. I gave this mother positive feedback and presented explanation of her choices in relation to Song-Song's development. Nee's confidence increased markedly as she transformed the empty room into an exciting, stimulating, and attractive venue.

Handling toys prior to intervention with a child, and making personal decisions which are based on an increase in understanding, empowers a parent and grants ownership and responsibility to the adult learner. Power which is gained from being a holder of knowledge relevant to a particular context can be transferred quickly, and effectively, from facilitator to parent. A formal pattern of teaching and learning in parenting sessions can rapidly progress and settle into an interactive rhythm which is founded on approach motivation.

Song-Song watched silently from his buggy, and rejected my attempts to converse by furrowing his eyebrows in response to my overtures. Nee looked upset and embarrassed at this rejection of my friendliness, and I explained how Song-Song's behaviour communicated his fear of this unknown set of circumstances. I asked Nee to respond to her son's trepidation and insecurity by creating a transition from the buggy, which represented Song-Song's secure environmental base, to the carpet of toys. Following this direction the mother gave her child part of an activity to hold as he sat and watched. She loosened his harness straps, and placed an adjoining piece on the floor nearby. A few moments after a beckoning of her hand, role-modelling of play, and positive body language which portrayed her belief in and expectation of Song-Song's participation, the little child had transitioned from his buggy into the session.

Together we communicated with the little boy through his mother's use of familial Mandarin communications, and my use of visual prompts which tapped into the child's curiosity and motivation.

Family learning

An assortment of activities had been carefully chosen to provide specific opportunities for interactive play:

- **Simple problem-solving toys below the child's current level of ability**
  This feature is useful to provide a quick return, and to attract a young child into a play session in unusual circumstances. Additionally, rapid achievement of a perceived "end" goal in a parenting session presents an anxious parent with an identifiable opportunity to recognise the process of attainment, to praise, and to empower her child.

  I find that parents are often reticent about using their voices on camera, and common barriers to communication are expressed universally by primary carers as awareness of accent, anxiety about the use of slang terms, concern over being too loud or too quiet, and not knowing what to say. Encouraging a parent and child to communicate effectively in the early stages of the session can make best use of the intervention, and promote fun in learning. Verbal role-modelling by a practitioner is key, and giving a parent actual phrases to copy in the initial stages are effective support mechanisms for the two generations of learners. Over time the parent should be encouraged to contribute "family words and expressions" which are familiar to the child. Recognisable terms, as used by an attachment figure, portray meaning, emotion, and links to the home environment. A positive attitude and interested tone has greater impact upon a young child's involvement in an activity than specific responses.

- **Complex problem-solving activities relating to the child's own interests**
  One aim of family early intervention is the increase of a child's and parent's involvement in learning and wellbeing during these processes. Involvement refers to the time spent on each activity, and the depth of learning achieved. Activities which reflect a child's current interests will extend interaction time, and increase motivation to achieve a goal or to use sensory exploration. A problem-solving activity such as threading wooden beads or shapes provides an easy opportunity for joint interaction with a parent. Parents demonstrate immense pride as

their little son or daughter uses eye–hand coordination. It is essential that the task is broken into composite parts to support in-depth learning by parents, and these interactions between practitioner and primary carer can be rich in knowledge and the promotion of understanding.

- **To speak or not to speak**
  Every parenting programme facilitator knows that parents often express that they do not wish to "disturb" a child who is playing quietly. However, interactive parenting takes the opposite approach. Children need to be informed of "positive play." Children's daily achievements should be recognised and acknowledged by the most significant person in their world. Affirmation from parent to child can take many different forms: verbal descriptive praise or signs (for example Makaton), gentle touch, thumbs-up gesture, smile, laughter, and copying child's actions. The communication represents the sentiment: "you are worthy and your contribution is valuable."

  The Positive Parenting Programme (Triple P) recommends that parents comment on behaviour that they "wish to see" (Sanders, 1999). Research shows that language acquisition supports cognitive development, and tracking a child's actions is paramount to this stage of learning (Vygotsky, 1986); however, too much stimulation, too many questions, and too many demands and suggestions by an adult can affect the brain's capacity, albeit in the short-term, to achieve a deep level of involvement. Video feedback is an ideal medium to demonstrate this cause-and-effect process to parents.

  To speak or not to speak. Periods of silence support take-up processes when the brain captures and retains knowledge by creating links with prior learning. All parents know their children's behaviour and reactions intimately, and the facilitator's role is to grant significance to the dance of reciprocity, and to respect each parent's knowledge and insight.

- **Obvious turn-taking activities**
  A fallen tower of wooden bricks can be quickly reassembled in order to sustain a child's attention, and minimise any feeling of failure. Supporting a parent with empathising with a child if the activity does not go to plan, and to promote shared humour, is a major contribution to building a foundation of resilience. Toys which are constructed of natural materials are gentle for young children to handle. Wood is kind to the touch of a small hand whether with the use of fine motor skills or in a plantar grasp. The properties of wood allow absorption of perspiration and nervous energy from an anxious learner which cannot be achieved with plastic artefacts.

- **Sensory stimulation and down-time**
  Sensory activities can be used to support a parent to introduce relaxation-time to a child, for example down-regulation of negative emotions by using an adult make-up brush to stroke pressure points such as wrists, ankles, behind the child's ears and neck, soles of the feet, and hands. Cool silk or brushed cotton can induce the same soporific effect which results in the child's increased awareness of internal physical wellbeing in association with positive emotions, and links to the adult attachment figure. These interactive interludes during play are essential to nurture, to consolidate, and to affirm a secure relationship. Knowing when and how to rest and relax during play is necessary for achievement of potential, and development of self-regulation.
- **Imaginative play**
  Toys which replicate small-world play do not need to be limited by a traditional doll's house and furniture but can also be represented by animals, puppets, mirrors, and books. Observing a child's breadth of imaginative play during parenting work provides a facilitator with comprehension of the experiences of the world which have been gained in the home environment. This knowledge and understanding is a platform for presentation of family learning.
- **Lift-the-flap book – a rich learning experience for parent and child**
  I recall many years ago in practice that we would hide pictures with our hand or the child's hands during the reading and sharing of books in order to stimulate curiosity and a learning partnership. A literary activity provides many opportunities for a child and adult to acquire the skills to watch, to wait, to anticipate, and to participate. The introduction of lift-the-flap books has facilitated these outcomes for early years workers and parents.

  The child and adult develop a shared understanding of processes and outcomes which supports self-regulation, both physically and emotionally; encourages concept linkage, fine motor skills, imaginative play, and communication; and creates a perfect atmosphere for the development of a parent–child relationship.
- **Play with recognisable boundaries and choices out of two**
  Social boundaries are essential for cooperative existence in small or large groups as children and adults. Choice-making can contribute effectively to the promotion of boundaries and supports the child in maintaining a sense of control over his or her world. This is useful for any child but essential for children who have experienced childhood adversities.

  Presenting a choice of two objects or two plans to a child emphasises the adult trust in a child's ability to achieve. It also minimises the child's dependency on adult-led behaviour management, and encourages decision-making and subsequent ownership of consequences.

These issues should be explained clearly to parents during play sessions and clarified through practical example. Supporting children in learning and in developing is challenging and complex due to the myriad of influences which affect neural connections, attitude, motivation, and recognition of attainment. Practitioners and facilitators of parenting programmes must gain comprehension of the multi-layers of learning in order to present this information effectively to primary carers.

- **Curiosity and motivation**
Play should present challenges to prompt curiosity and further exploration. Opportunities should be given to consolidate learning but also to seek out stimulation and deeper comprehension. Simple strategies such as the use of chiffon scarves, clear plastic pockets, material bags, drawstring bags, and containers with screw tops or snap-on lids can be effective. Objects can be hidden in sight but out of reach initially – using a chiffon scarf as a light, removable cover, tucking a tiny item into the bottom corner of a clear plastic pocket – then hidden – within an easily opened bag with the drawstring loosened – and then eventually secured – using a container. In this way, exploration is encouraged through promotion of sound, emotional investment, and positive anticipation of the unknown. This leads to approach motivation, active independent participation, and a higher level of learning.

Current research recommends a trauma-informed approach to interventions which are implemented in a context of childhood adversities. Six principles are regularly promoted in literature and curricular guidance, and these aspects will be discussed throughout the next chapters on relationships, environment, and pedagogy. The six principles are safety, trustworthiness and transparency, peer support, collaboration and mutuality, empowerment, voice and choice, and finally cultural, historical, and gender issues (Smith, 2018).

As previously mentioned in this chapter an attachment relationship with a primary carer provides a base for a child to learn about his or her sense of self, to observe and interact with the proximal and distal environment, and to gain motivation and curiosity to seek out knowledge and understanding. The next chapter will extend the discussion on adversities and learning by exploring the role of attachment figures in response to tolerable and toxic stress.

References

Allen, G. 2011, *Early intervention: The next steps*, CSJ and Smith Institute, London.
Bearer, E.L. & Mulligan, B.S. 2018, 'Epigenetic changes associated with early life experiences: Saliva, a bio-specimen for DNA methylation signatures', *Current Genomics*, vol. 19, no. 8, pp. 8. viewed 28 March, 2019, https:ncbi.nlm.nih.gov/pubmed/30532647.

24 Adverse childhood experiences

Bellazaire, A. 2018, 'Preventing and mitigating the effects of adverse childhood experiences', National conference of state legislatures, viewed 1 January, 2019, www.ncsl.org.

Bellis, M.A., Hughes, K., Leckenby, N., Jones, L., Baban, A., Kachaeva, M., Povilaitis, R., Pudule, I., Qirjako, G., Ulukol, B., Raleva, M. & Terzic, N. 2014, 'Adverse childhood experiences and associations with health-harming behaviours in young adults: Surveys in eight eastern European countries', *Bulletin of the World Health Organisation*, vol. 92, no. 9, pp. 641–55. DOI: 10.2471/BLT.13.129247.

Bowlby, J. 1979, *The making and breaking of affectional bonds*. Routledge, Abingdon, pp. 140–141.

Bright, M.A., Alford, S.M., Hinojosa, M.S., Knapp, C. & Fernandez-Baca, D.E. 2014, 'Adverse childhood experiences and dental health in children and adolescents', *Community Dentistry and Oral Epidemiology*. DOI: 10.1111/cdoe.12137.

Cardoso, J., Almeida, T., Ramos, C. & Sousa, S. 2018, 'Relationship between childhood trauma and sleep disturbances: The role of perceived stress as a mediator', *Journal of Aggression, Maltreatment and Trauma*, vol. 27, no. 10. DOI: 10.1080/10926771.2018.1501628.

Children's Bureau. 2018, 'Adverse childhood experiences', viewed 26 December, 2018, https://childwelfare.gov/topics/preventing/preventionmonth/resources/ace/.

Day, S., Douglas, H. & Johnson, R. 2017, *Solihull approach; understanding trauma*. NHS Foundation Trust, Birmingham.

Devaney, J. & Duffy, M. 2017, 'Post-traumatic stress disorder and childhood maltreatment', viewed 10 June, 2017, https://nspcc.org.uk/services-and-resources/impact-evidence-evaluation-child-pri.

Di Lemma, L.C.G., Davies, A.R., Ford, K., Hughes, K., Homolova, L., Gray, B. & Richardson, G. 2019, *Responding to adverse childhood experiences – an evidence review of interventions to prevent and address adversity across the life-course*, Public Health Wales NHS Trust, Cardiff.

Edwards, D. 2018, *Childhood sexual abuse and brain development: A discussion of associated structural changes and negative psychological outcomes*, DOI: 10.1002/car.2514.

Felitti, V.J., Anda, R.F., Nordenberg, D., Williamson, D.F., Spitz, A.M., Edwards, V., Koss, M.P. & Marks, J.S. 1998, 'Relationships of childhood abuse and household dysfunction to many of the leading causes of death in adults', *American Journal of Preventive Medicine*, vol. 14, no. 4. viewed 25 December, 2017, https://nhs.scot.knowledge.network.

Foundation for Environmental Education (FEE). 2015, 'Eco-Schools Programme', viewed 31 March, 2019, https://en.unesco.org/greencitizens/stories/eco-schools-programme.

House of Commons Health & Social Care Committee. 2019, 'First 1000 days of life', viewed 27 February, 2019, www.parliament.uk/hsccom.

Landor, M., Kennedy, H. & Todd, L. 2010, 'Video interaction guidance as a method to promote secure attachment', *Educational and Child Psychology*, vol. 27, no. 3. viewed 31 March, 2019, https://nhs.scot.knowledge.network.

Larkin, H., Felittis, V.J. & Anda, R. 2014, 'Social work and adverse childhood experiences, research: Implications for practice and health policy', viewed 30 March, 2019, https://researchgate.net/publication/258280317.

McLaughlin, K. 2017, 'The long shadow of adverse childhood experiences', *Psychological Science Agenda/April 2017/Science Brief*, viewed 1 December, 2018, https:americanpsychologicalsociety.

National Scientific Council on the Developing Child. 2011, 'The science of resilience', *The Inbrief Series*. viewed 21 June, 2018, https://developingchild.harvard.edu/science/key-concepts/resilience.

National Scientific Council on the Developing Child. 2016, 'From best practices to breakthrough impacts', viewed 21 June, 2018, https://developingchild.harvard.edu.

National Scientific Council on the Developing Child. 2018, *Understanding motivation: building the brain architecture that supports learning, health, and community participation, working paper no. 14*, viewed 1 January, 2019, http://developingchild.harvard.edu.

The National Institute for Health and Care Excellence. (NICE). 2017, 'Child abuse and neglect: NICE guideline', viewed 10 October, 2017, nice.org.uk/guidance/ng76.

Palm, G. & Cooke, B. 2018, 'Parent education and family life education: a critical link in early childhood education policy', *National Council on Family Relations Policy Brief*, vol. 3, no. 2. viewed 1 August, 2018, www.ncfr.org.

Perry, B. 2014, 'Helping traumatized children, a brief overview for caregivers', viewed 3 March, 2019, www.ChildTrauma.org.

Royal College of Paediatrics and Child Health. 2019, 'State of child health – Scotland two years on', viewed 31 January, 2019, http://rcpch.ac.uk/state-of-child-. Health.

Sanders, M.R. 1999, 'Triple P-positive parenting program: towards an empirically validated multilevel parenting and family support strategy for the prevention of behaviour and emotional problems in children', *Clinical Child and Family Psychology Review*, vol. 2, no. 2. Plenum Publishing Corporation, New York, pp. 71–90.

Scottish Government. 2017, *Mental health strategy 2017–2017*, Scottish Government, Edinburgh.

Scottish Government. 2018, *Getting it right for every child (GIRFEC)*, Scottish Government, Edinburgh.

Sethi, D., Yon, Y., Parekh, N., Anderson, T., Huber, J., Rakovac, I. & Meinck, F. 2018, *European status report on preventing child maltreatment*, World Health Organisation, Denmark.

Shonkoff, J.P. & Fisher, P. 2013, 'Re-thinking evidence-based practice and two-generation programmes to create the future of early childhood policy', *Developmental Psychology*, 1635–53. November 25. viewed 1 December, 2018, www.healthscotland.scot.

Smith, L. 2018, *Adverse childhood experiences (ACEs): educational interventions*, The Institute for Research and Innovation in Social Services (Iriss), Glasgow.

Vygotsky, L. 1986, *Thought and language*, The Massachusetts Institute of Technology, Baskerville.

Whitters, H.G. 2018, *Family learning to inclusion: theory, practice, and partnerships*, Routledge, Abingdon. pp. 20–3.

Whitters, H.G. 2019, *Attainment and executive functioning in the early years: research and inclusive practice for lifelong learning*, Routledge, Abingdon.

2 Attachment

This chapter reviews the significance of an attachment figure for a child's ability and capacity to learn. Information will be discussed by focusing upon the biological and emotional effects, with particular emphasis on the catalytic impact of a secure status upon a child's exploration. This chapter will present the reader with an opportunity to consider the intrinsic links between the internal impact of adversity and attachment, and external representation through behaviour and actions.

Example from practice

Adidja has stayed in her new nursery for the first time without her primary carer who is her father, Neche. The little girl's body and mind have been alert to his absence for the last 60 minutes or 3,600 seconds. As each second passes stress can be experienced by a child who is "settling" into an unfamiliar environment, albeit one that offers a positive opportunity for play and development. Adidja was uncertain if her father would return. Key workers confidently reassure children of this commitment from their parents; however, no prior experience of separation can adequately prepare young children for the transition from home to educational setting without an attachment figure.

Adidja is exhausted; then a noise is heard and her father fills the doorframe with his presence. Neche made an entrance which was noticed by many other children as, arms outstretched, he took long strides across the play-room to his daughter. Adidja did not move but watched. Neche lifted the two-year-old and pulled her towards him to reaffirm their relationship, but Adidja was confused. Her presentation emulated the reaction of many children which I have observed on countless occasions in early years settings, during access visits, and in hospitals.

Adidja held tentatively onto her father's brown leather jacket, breathed deeply as his scent transported her emotions to home, and turned her head away. Adidja kept her eyes averted, and head turned to one side, facing away from her father. This human pose can be seen in a multitude of contexts, and communicates our need for attachment and reassurance, and our uncertainty through separation. Daily examples occur throughout our cultures which may be witnessed directly or watched speculatively on our television screens: at a harbour's edge as service-men and -women meet and greet their partners after a long absence, on the railway platform as parents collect their children from boarding school as summer holidays commence, in hospital casualty departments as distant relatives attempt to support one another, and at airports as family members reunite following international disasters.

As human beings we need to be securely attached, and we want to be loved, but circumstances can challenge our interpretation and understanding of our emotional status. Does the separation indicate a change in our attachment? As professionals we strive to comprehend and to support this inherent need for children throughout the world.

Attachment

Attachment was described as "the bond which ties" by John Bowlby (1969). Bowlby and his colleague James Robertson, and latterly Mary Ainsworth, were pioneers in the study of attachment between child and mother: conducting research, comprehending the theoretical significance to human development, and communicating their findings for practical use.

The legacy of knowledge from Bowlby, Robertson, and Ainsworth is far-reaching. Practitioners, undergraduates, postgraduates, and researchers in many disciplines have learned about attachment theory and gained insight into human relationships. However, over years of teaching and practising, I have become aware that interpretation of this theory into practice focuses upon comprehension of **secure** attachment. Professionals understand the effect of a consistent, significant adult in the formation of an imaginary circle of security which enables a child to explore his or her world, to learn, and to develop. The *circle of security* is depicted clearly in pictorial format by Cooper et al. (2000).

Training and experience can enable key workers to identify with this role and define their responsibilities towards the children in their care. We write dissertations on attachment as we aim to achieve our vocational career, and graduate with a commitment to fulfil this need for children in their earliest years; however, greater insight needs to be sought and used to inform practice (Whitters, 2017). From a knowledge base of secure attachment it can be challenging for practitioners to extrapolate, and to comprehend, the effects of insecure attachment. The rationale of daily practice in the early years is positivity, attainable achievement, and a "can do" attitude.

The knowledge base of **insecure** attachment by practitioners tends to be represented at the practice level by description of negative behaviours which are described as *resistance to social boundaries* and often colloquially expressed as "he will not do as he is told…" Responses which are based upon this premise grant power to the adult, and the young learner develops dependency on adult-regulation of his behaviour and potentially his emotions. These interventional strategies bypass the adversities which influenced a chain of events within the child, and led to actualisation of his behaviour in the external social world.

Attachment and attachment disorders

There continues to be confusion regarding definitions and comprehension of **secure/insecure attachment** and **attachment disorders**. Secure or insecure attachment is predominantly relationship-specific, and the pattern of interpersonal interactions can change over time. Alternatively attachment disorders refer to two rare forms of diagnosable mental disorder which are termed "reactive" or "disinhibited" (Turner et al., 2019). Behaviours associated with these mental disorders tend to be demonstrated consistently across all care-giving relationships although the child's expression of the relationship may alter with maturity.

Turner et al. (2019) report that 50% of children who are in care meet the criteria for diagnosis of a psychiatric disorder which compares to 10% of children who remain with their birth family throughout childhood. This research team comments on the difficulty in clinical diagnoses of attachment disorder, autistic spectrum disorder, and attention deficit hyperactivity disorder as symptoms can appear to overlap. In my experience parents seek out information via internet resources, and primary carers are often directed to sites by clinicians. From the parental perspective matching a child's symptoms and behaviours to a check-list, and vice-versa, can frequently lead to misinterpretation by carers, and subsequently a negative attitude towards a child's progress and achievement of potential.

In recent years paediatricians have been seeking contributions for diagnostic evidence from practitioners in early years settings and school, in addition to parental description, home videos, and explanation of a child's behaviours. The use of multi-disciplinary expertise, and multi-modal information, is invaluable in creating a holistic case history of each child in a range of environments, and within contexts of different relationships.

This chapter focuses upon secure/insecure attachment. I often encounter a lack of understanding of internal processes, and a weakness in interpretation of frameworks, which can close the implementation gap from theory to practice in the field. Bowlby's earliest works clearly present the effects of personal trauma as experienced during mother and child separation (Bowlby, 1998). Emphasis is given to supporting internal change in order to influence external presentation in the form of behaviour and actions. The catalyst is emotional reaction; therefore in order to comprehend the practitioner's role we have to focus upon each child's communication of his emotions.

A common practical example of these circumstances is an approach to behaviour management. Promotion of positive behaviour is complex, and involves changing human behaviour from two perspectives: internal understanding and inner working model, on one hand; and, on the other, external expression in the form of actions (what we do), behaviour (how we do it), and emotions (how we feel). The two perspectives need to be connected in order for the child to gain an understanding of self:

1. The child has to be made aware of her current emotion, and associated actions, in order to increase her comprehension and inform her inner working model.
2. The social boundary which is applicable to the context has to be communicated clearly to the child. Environmental cues are essential to effective management of behaviour and promotion of self-regulation. Rules of play should be apparent and easily communicable through prompts and role-modelling. If practitioners in a play-room are frequently debating the rules and patterns of acceptable play then it may be that these social cues are not obvious to the children.

Example from practice

Peggy and Masood are ascending the wooden bars of the climbing frame, sitting down carefully, and sliding with arms held aloft and wide, just like an aeroplane. Masood decides to develop his play, and the turn-taking pattern between the two four-year-olds changes. Masood copies a prompt from his key worker and folds his arms at the top of the slide. It is challenging and exciting to balance without the use of arms as rudders for your body! This delay of a few minutes has upset Peggy's routine and expectations. She kicks Masood's back as he, poised intrepidly, positions himself at the launch site at the top of the slide.

The little girl needs reminding of the social rules, support in regulating her behaviour in this new context, comprehension and prompting to change her expectations of Masood's actions, and support in adapting and increasing her executive functioning (Whitters, 2019).

Body language can effectively support a child's understanding of social rules. It is essential that body language and verbal reminder from adult to child do not impose a threat or bring anger, but rather be an age-appropriate communication strategy to educate the child and to reconfigure her frame of reference. Learning does not occur effectively in an atmosphere of adult power, control, and coercion. We are teaching children to understand and to regulate their own behaviour and actions.

The key worker tapped Peggy's shoes, then Masood's back, as she acknowledged the child's emotions, tracked her actions, and shook her head as she communicated the social boundary quietly and calmly. This body language gave confirmation to the little four-year-old girl that her behaviour was not appropriate.

A lowering of voice volume is far more effective than raising of voice in response to negative behaviour. An adult who uses a loud angry voice has adopted the child's emotions, and sends a clear message through role-modelling that a negative attitude is appropriate to the context.

The sequence of responses during behaviour management does not need to happen quickly in order to allow an immediate return to the activity. Promotion of positive behaviour is invaluable to our conduct throughout life. Take time, hold the child's hands, compose your own emotions, await the child's eye-contact, and relay the boundary in a statement of fact. These strategies portray knowledge and promote understanding to the learner: "Peggy, your friend is not for kicking" is a useful alternative to, "No, no, no, no kicking!" The child's name should always precede learning experiences.

*Now for the education – "Peggy, **wait instead**. One... two... three... your turn." The key worker held up her hand to promote waiting. This action gives the child an opportunity to gain control and inhibit actions. If an adult physically restrains a child then he or she becomes dependent on external regulation, and will probably push against the adult as opposed to restraining forward movement; however, most children do learn incrementally, and it may be that physical reminders are necessary initially, followed by visual and verbal prompting.*

The expected outcome is simple – Peggy has to wait a few extra seconds to allow Masood to develop his play – but the internal processes which are taking place in Peggy are sophisticated. The key worker used a well-tried childcare strategy of finger-counting to delay an action. Wait, one and two and three, then she gradually raised her voice volume and smiled broadly in recognition of Peggy's achievement.

A quiet calm voice in response to negative behaviours, followed by a gradual raising of voice level which indicates positive anticipation and leads the child forward by using empowering phrases, can support a child to pause and to commence self-regulation. The human voice and use of body language are sophisticated tools which can successfully guide young people to learn, to understand, and to take responsibility for themselves. These tools are accessible to every educator for use as required. It is important to know your own capabilities well, and to hone your skills so as to be ready for action.

Ultimately acknowledgement of an end goal should be given with regard to the child's change of actions and emotions in this context of promoting positive behaviour. It is essential to use strategies which are significant to each child, for example a high-five hand-clap, thumbs-up sign, broad smile, gentle touch to the child's face, or quick hug and arm around his shoulders. The child's inner working model is re-configured: what he does, how he does it, and how he feels are immersed in positivity and remembered in this context.

Encouraging repetition of the newly acquired behaviour and skills is essential for the child to recall the sequence, and retain neural links from memory to action. Implicit memory is influenced by the positive emotions experienced by Peggy during these learning sequences, and explicit memory is based upon her current interest of the climbing frame and slide.

These simplistic examples occur frequently in the early years stage and provide a foundation for life skills which are often required in adolescence. It is during the teenage years that potentially adverse situations, peer pressure, and choice-making are prevalent.

The children were united again, a team of two learners, and the key worker demonstrated relief and satisfaction that she had reacted so positively to the situation. As professionals we do not always access the "optimum" approach. We are also affected by emotions and by our physical and mental wellbeing, and , by a multitude of influences on professional time; however, we need to recognise a learning arena, a child's readiness to absorb knowledge, and to capitalise upon each opportune moment.

The mandate is always to replace the negative with a positive – educate, educate, educate at every opportunity. The child retains her pride and she has re-configured her reference framework for social play, and the shared moments of achievement have been embraced by Peggy, Masood, and key worker.

John Bowlby

Background

John Bowlby was born in 1907. By the time of his death in 1990, this pioneer in childcare and education had created a wealth of knowledge and understanding which is treasured by professionals today, and which benefits children globally.

Bowlby's childhood experiences included receiving care by a nursery nurse in the family home alongside his five siblings. At the age of nine, John Bowlby attended boarding school. Bowlby initially studied at the University of Cambridge, and subsequently entered University College Hospital in London, and graduated in medicine. The young Bowlby was following in his father's footsteps by pursuing a medical career although Bowlby senior was a renowned surgeon to the royal family of that time. Thereafter, John Bowlby specialised in child psychiatry and psycho-analysis at the Maudsley Hospital, and the majority of his research was conducted within employment at the Tavistock Clinic in London (Tizard, 2009).

Bowlby had a great thirst for learning and an early interest in understanding the behaviour of human beings, particularly during times of adversity. Throughout his career this psycho-analyst perused the thinking of contemporaries, and developed his own theories over time. As early as the 1940s Bowlby's research was linking childhood adversities, particularly in the earliest years, to emotional trauma and associated behaviours in adolescence and adulthood. Bowlby's training in adult mental health and his research in the context of young children gave him a broad knowledge of human development to use in gaining deeper understanding of behaviours and causes. This researcher's rationale was determining preventative measures to support attainment of the individual, and impact upon the good of wider society as children entered adulthood. Within many of his publications Bowlby referred to circumstances of specific children and it was clear that the researcher was invested in the children's wellbeing, and that his life's work was grounded in supporting the vulnerable in achieving.

Bowlby's research

Integral to the foundation of Bowlby's research on attachment between child and mother was the work of his colleague, James Robertson. In 1948, Bowlby and Robertson conducted a study on the effect of maternal separation upon a young child's personality (Bowlby, 1969). The research was based on the assumption that a mother or mother-figure is regarded as a necessary secure base during the formative years of childhood; therefore, loss of this individual is a dominant factor in emotional developmental delay, and impactful upon personality.

Bowlby and Robertson concluded that the behaviours and reactions of young children were similar to the behaviour observed in adults who had experienced separation in early childhood. It seems that the impact of early adversities could be retained, and continue to be demonstrated in some individuals throughout the lifespan. These researchers describe the profound emotional impact which observations of these distressed children had, and they were motivated and determined to inform academia and practice. A crucial decision was made to investigate the pathological processes by researching the effects of separation *and* reconciliation. In 1950 the World Health Organisation commissioned Bowlby to research the mental health of children who were spending all, or some, of their childhood in residential care.

Interestingly, Bowlby wrote in his final report that his research findings agreed with the thinking of previous researchers – a young child requires a secure attachment relationship to learn and develop. Additionally, Bowlby highlighted a lack of evidence on the processes which contribute to "maternal deprivation," and subsequently the impact upon the internal workings of the infant (Bowlby, 1998). Seventy years later we continue to seek out understanding of these issues.

Attachment theory was published in the 1960s by Bowlby and Mary Ainsworth (Bowlby, 1998). Ainsworth had developed an approach, termed "The Strange Situation," to investigating behaviours and emotions before and after short separations from the mother-figure. The findings contributed to categorisations of attachment status; however, Ainsworth significantly refers to the individual nature of children's responses.

As an undergraduate student I studiously learned the definitions of each category of attachment, but I was also puzzled by the different reactions of children in common circumstances, particularly siblings. I observed in nursery play-rooms, and noted much overlapping of attachment behaviours of children which could be located within more than one category. At this stage I began to consider the influence of context, emotional status at a point in time, and significantly the different relationships which a child could create with a variety of adults.

Thirty years ago these tentative ideas were often dismissed by workplace mentors but today's students are regarded as educational pioneers who support mentors to blend the old and the new. I often envy the free access which students have to multiple data-bases incorporating research from every country and culture. As a practice-mentor I welcome students to the service, and actively seek out fresh interpretations of issues from the perspective of a younger generation. We are all learners.

A key feature of attachment theory is the influence from a child's earliest attachment models upon the creation of future relationships; however, recognition also has to be given to the unique interpretation and reactions to adversities which are encountered throughout life. During subsequent research, and multiple publications, Bowlby revised his initial warnings about the long-lasting effect of childhood adversities, and indicated the value of intervention, and the adaptability of the human being if conditions were appropriate. Neuroscience has offered an explanation of Bowlby's beliefs, and gives us evidence of brain plasticity throughout the lifespan. Brain scans have shown the forming of different neural pathways in the brain following injury or trauma, and the ability and capacity of human beings to adapt in order to continue the processes of learning and developing (Moore et al., 2017).

In 1988, Bowlby advised future researchers to study the effects of internal and external influences in order to further this exploration of human development (Tizard, 2009). The challenges for governments in understanding and responding to adverse effects upon a population, and for practitioners in comprehending the individual's reaction and interpretation to personal circumstances, remain today. There is a current impetus for society to take responsibility for childhood adversities, and provide rehabilitation in an appropriate format throughout the lifespan (Bellazaire, 2018).

Bretherton and Munholland (2016) express that the attachment system is activated by actual or potential threat. The rationale of this genetic response in humans appears to be based on survival of the individual, and ultimately continuation of the species. Over the last 30 years I have noticed that the attachment figure is increasingly accessed by a child for two purposes:

1. To remove or minimise the effect of a threat, including the transition period from primary carer to secondary attachment figure.
2. To provide affirmation of achievement.

The second point, to provide affirmation of achievement, has emerged through a change in expectations of the relationship between a child and an adult, whether parent or professional. The approach to rearing children has evolved in the United Kingdom and elsewhere, and far greater emphasis is placed on positive interactions between adult and child. Interactions focus upon the promotion of a nurturing environment, input of learning, and recognition of child's current base of knowledge and emotional status, as opposed to developmental expectations.

Acknowledgement is given to the child's sense of self, and the impact from a secure attachment relationship. This culture change has informed inclusive practice, parenting in the home, and expectations by society. The child's brain is certainly not regarded as the tabula rasa described by John Locke 330 years ago (Locke, 2019) but rather an independent active contributor who operates in a context of at least one secure attachment relationship. A baby has a myriad of genetic possibilities at birth which are ready to be realised rapidly, or to remain dormant for many years until the correct conditions surmise, or to be passed tacitly to the next generation, or to atrophy over time for evermore.

Inner working model

Bowlby (1998) describes development of the inner working model as encompassing:

- Reflection upon knowledge past and current.
- Consideration of potential eventualities.
- Assessment of responses, and attitude of an attachment figure.

This model guides actions, behaviours, and emotions, and continues to evolve throughout our lives; therefore each child's perspectives of external and internal influences will change as determinants in decision-making have a greater or lesser effect. If a child's behaviour is regulated by an adult then this process is incorporated within the inner working model as a condition for action. Previous authors apply the term *attribution* to describe the working model as actively changing through an increase in understanding, as opposed to simply reflecting reality (Bretherton & Munholland, 2016).

It seems that the inner working model represents a subjective viewpoint which reflects, and may emulate, the influences from an attachment figure, and potentially the wider social context. The research of Bretherton and Munholland (2016) also indicated that the presence (or absence) of the mother promotes (or removes) the child's feeling of security in an environmental context. Young children, who have not yet developed the theory of mind, are unable to consider extenuating circumstances which affect their attachment figure. For example, if a mother has a cold, and appears irritable, then the infant will have a lower emotional resilience to her negative attitude than his mature sibling who appreciates his mother's temporary incapacity. Sensitivity and emotional availability, *most of the time*, are key attributes to secure attachment and effective parenting. "Good enough parenting" is the goal that we aspire to achieve.

Children are profoundly affected by the interpretation of, and reactions to, the external world by their attachment figure. Another influence is the carer's responses to the child's expression of his internal processes as demonstrated by his behaviour and emotions. Potential for a circle of security is inextricably associated with the attitude and reactions of a primary carer. There are multiple opportunities within early years services to expose children to unfamiliar and educative experiences. The child's preliminary reaction is often influenced by perceptions which may have formed prior to attendance in a service, in a context of adversities in childhood.

Childhood aggression

Many researchers and practitioners would agree that physical childhood aggression peaks at around two years of age. Aggression in the early years signifies a child's long- or short-term inability to effectively communicate emotions and needs. Anti-social physical behaviours can also indicate a lack of maturity in interpretation of an unfamiliar situation, and incapacity to predict and to accommodate the actions of others who are usually in close proximity.

Executive functioning requires the use of working memory, response inhibition, and attention-/task-shifting (Pauen & EDOS, 2016). Set-shifting is the most complicated of the components which relies upon the use of memory and skills to inhibit actions. A positive outcome depends upon Peggy recognising that her actions need to change in response to her peer (Whitters, 2019).

Fonagy (2003) suggests that violence is an inherent attribute of human beings which can be minimised by social influences. The research indicates that violent tendencies can be reduced through role-modelling by an attachment figure, the promotion of social expectations, and ultimately the raising of self-esteem, communication skills, and the theory of mind – supporting a child to develop a sense of the autobiographical self. Fonagy highlights the mother-figure as key to shifting the child's aggressive behaviour. Role-modelling from an attachment figure is essential to *mentalisation* as termed by Fonagy (2003); therefore it is important that the promotion of positive behaviour in services, and at home, is implemented in a context of secure attachment relationships.

Interestingly, Fonagy mentions guilt as a self-limiting influence upon a child's negativity. This level of understanding regarding personal responsibility, ownership of actions, and social expectations requires a mature sense of self which is not realised in the earliest years of childhood.

Almost 20 years ago, research was conducted by using a sample set of over 1,000 children to study potential predictors of persistent physical aggression in boys (Nagin & Tremblay, 2001). The findings indicated that boys with a high level of aggression in early years services were most likely to demonstrate chronic violence over time. As a practitioner I am always delighted when data reflects my knowledge of daily practice in the field. The research team had recorded an example of pro-social behaviour which can be observed in any service throughout the world; a child picking up an object which has been dropped by another person, and returning it to the rightful owner. I have often shared similar examples of executive functioning to parents during feedback sessions, and described their child's behaviour as demonstrating the early stages of empathy.

The study showed similarities between adversities which were experienced by both generations – parents and children (Nagin & Tremblay, 2001). Conclusions reported that mothers could be the agents who perpetuate the cycle of aggressive retort. It is well-known that the inter-play of influences from genetics and environment are complicated to determine, and may be impossible to isolate, but current parenting programmes encompass family learning and target change and development in more than one generation (Whitters, 2018).

Research on biological processes has contributed profoundly to our knowledge and understanding of attachment which includes links to growth, intellect, and mental and physical wellbeing in infanthood (Shirvanian & Michael, 2017), as well as the longer-term impact from consistent access to a secure base upon which to learn and achieve throughout the lifespan.

Schore (2015) describes correlation from close contact interactions between carer and infant through an increase in dopamine, and subsequent growth in the right hemisphere of the brain. Physical contact is an instinctive practical response to care-giving, and research promoted by Howes et al. (1998) looked at this topic in a context of services. A positive correlation was identified between an increase in a child's secure attachment, and programmes which supported an increase in a care-giver's sensitivity. Notably a *lack* of reciprocity was linked to an increase in cortisol, termed "the stress hormone," and subsequent physical and mental ill-health.

The skills and actions linked with reflective functioning are communicated to children within nurturing contexts in early years services, and within the implementation of specific interventions, for example, the Circle of Security Project (Marvin et al., 2002). In order to promote reflection, which is closely associated with executive functioning, the adult carer needs to understand his own sense of self. The ability to recognise disruption to the attachment relationship, and to repair the rupture, are key aspects in the creation of a secure and consistent bond between adult and child. Previous authors have identified the significance of participants in a relationship, whether child and parent or child and carer, in interpreting and responding to each other's cues and signals. Miscuing by parents may be based upon their own childhood experiences, and can perpetuate avoidant attachment.

Example from practice

> *Hafiz is lying on a large comfortable bean bag. When this artefact was purchased staff termed the colour as taupe, and described the soft, warm brushed-velvet cushion as the "chillax" area. The children quickly applied the term "brown mushroom," and each day two or three youngsters climb on board and share this centre-piece in their busy play-room: resting, chatting, or simply perusing their environment from a lofty height.*
>
> *Hafiz is three years old. She is lying spread-eagled on her back, looking at the hanging mobiles above her head – shiny CD discs, paper towel tubes, strands of pleated coloured wool, and laminated pages*

from a discarded nursery book – all up-cycled in the eco-tradition. Her mother, Salima, enters the area. Hafiz opens her eyes wider, her pupils dilate, and she sends urgent tacit signals to her attachment figure, "I am here, pick me up, I need you!" Hafiz's desire for reassurance escalates and although her body is tired her emotions are alert, and actively seeking confirmation of secure attachment.

Salima glances at her daughter and comments to the general playroom, "See, she does not want to come with me." The young mother deftly straightens her gold embroidered head-scarf, and turns towards the doorway. Her light perfume lingers and wafts in the direction of Hafiz. The little girl increases her signalling, and gives a forlorn cry: the ubiquitous noise that every young human and animal can make in the moment of abandonment.

The bean-bag is all enveloping, and Hafiz struggles to respond to this crisis as her mother walks towards the play-room exit. Salima's walk portrays anger and frustration. She has missed the cues of attachment. She has not interpreted the signals. She has not reflected in time to consider her daughter's needs, and her actions have created a rupture in the mother–daughter relationship which will have to be repaired.

Simple, common daily actions can have potentially life-changing consequences if repeated over time. It is well-documented that self-regulation in children is dependent on positive care-giving to minimise tolerable stress, and to input positive interactions which contribute towards the creation of a sustainable attachment relationship (Cambridge Core, 2017).

Secure attachment in early years services

Attachment is complex, and incorporates the use of cues, signals, verbal and physical prompts, and expectations which may be linked to culture, family values, or organisational policy. One goal of the Circle of Security project is supporting parents in comprehending the change from defensive actions to empathic responding (Marvin et al., 2002). The cycles of rupture *and* repair, *and* attunement with a secure attachment figure, can contribute to resilience in young children, and developmental competence.

Emotional awareness and cognition should be partnered in learning, and support child and parent in adapting and in embracing changes in order to develop. Van der Kolk (2003) warns that "disturbed children" can be a consequence of interpretation through cognition per se *or* understanding which is solely based upon emotion. In order to support comprehension of parents, an analogy of children's physical development and brain development can be shared.

- Practice in using muscles during play will shape and extend your child's physical motor skills, and the promotion of rich learning experiences will influence his or her cognition and emotional wellbeing.

Children who have experienced trauma will often interpret, and react to, everyday situations from this cognitive and emotional base of knowledge. Secure attachment is the catalyst which supports the child to "be ready" for learning, to actively seek out new experiences, and to re-configure the inner working model. Past and current research emphasises the importance of nurture as an expression of human attachment, with particular regard to physical touch and love (Campbell-Barr et al., 2015; Evans, 2019; Malcolm, 2019; Van der Kolk, 2003). Feeling secure through nurturing experiences supports a child in minimising the pattern of stress responses which he has acquired in relation to trauma. Slowly the inner working model begins to change.

Research which was conducted in 2014 indicated a link between attachment, environment, and executive functioning (Fay-Stammbach et al., 2014). This literature review discusses significant influences from each family's culture which affect parental input to socio-cognitive development in the home, and ultimately the child's expression of his knowledge and understanding.

Elfer and Page (2015) also studied influences on attachment from the environment by focusing upon early years services. Conclusions highlighted "contradictions" and "confusion" caused by differences in professional knowledge and understanding, and personal beliefs about children in a care organisation. Data was collected from eight nursery managers and indicated the importance of each professional's interpretation of his role, and the status of a baby in the same context.

The findings presented two opposing interpretations: a baby is regarded as a vulnerable dependent being, or a competent active agent. Data from establishments which adhered to the same or similar policies was found to inform the two categories inconsistently, and observations of practice differed from recorded interviews with participants.

Although the participant group was small, three key factors did emerge from this research:

1. Attachment to a key person is grounded in early years pedagogy.
2. Publication of curricula for under threes over the last 20 years has promoted teaching and learning in the early years context.
3. Increased opportunities to develop socially are recognised as important to the young infant in a care service.

Conclusions indicated that attachment in the home environment is relevant to specific family culture, but attachment in a service is a response to the baby's fluctuating emotional needs, in addition to supporting executive functioning (Elfer & Page, 2015). Personal *and* professional beliefs appeared to affect the perceptions of the nursery managers. It was clear that participants felt confused regarding the role of a nursery, and the practical implementation of responsibilities with regard to attachment relationships, expectations of parents, and promotion of learning for recorded curricular outcomes.

In my experience this lack of clarity is common in early years establishments. Introduction of formal curricula can maintain consistency of service delivery, and ultimately support inclusion policies within services, and throughout a nation; however, practitioners express that pre-determined plans can impact upon responsive implementation of care and education to individual children. Regulatory systems do impose undue pressures upon workplaces, and can result in professional adversities.

Intervention

Records of employment throughout the world demonstrate a steady increase in the numbers of working mothers, for example, in Australia 81% in 2009 compared to 71% ten years earlier (Shirvanian & Michael, 2017). More children are spending informative years in the care of services. Alongside these insights comes an increase in accountability for practitioners in the early years who are repeatedly informed of the significance of the learning period from pre-birth to three years. Geoffroy et al. (2007) has indicated that nurturing and education from practitioners can compensate for lack of appropriate parental care.

Strategic decision-making by governments can result in innovative approaches to supporting vulnerable families. In 2017, the United Kingdom government launched a national Reducing Parent Conflict programme in a context of intervention in the child's early years (Pote et al., 2019). It is known that family learning promotes change in several generations, and contributes effectively to sustaining a positive lifestyle without intensive input by services. Targeting parent conflict in order to maintain a couple's relationship is an interesting approach, and is based upon the creation of a nuclear family as a base for the child's development, and achievement of potential. Previous philosophies supported mothers *or* fathers, who had unattainable relationships, to be the main sole carers of their children, or to create a shared care plan.

Many studies recommend training and development of attachment-based practice for professionals who work in childcare and education. A comparative study by Murray et al., (2018) explored parent–practitioner relationships in the early years. The findings indicated more differences than similarities between the participating countries of England, Hungary, and Kazakhstan. Each cultural context was significant to the parent's and child's development; therefore a professional knowledge skill base was not necessarily transferrable between the three countries.

Knowledge is easy to share but weak without comprehension of practice. Relationship-based practice is led by the policies, procedures, and culture of an organisation; however, within each play-room, or school-class, practice represents the subjective response of each professional. Personal reflection, and the ability to critique oneself, are essential characteristics for professional development, in addition to consideration of the unique attributes and needs of individual children.

Complex trauma

Complex trauma is regarded as a child's exposure to one or more traumatic events, and the resultant short- or long-term impact. The financial and emotional cost to the individual and to society has been recognised by governments throughout the world, and the associative issues are current political topics.

The American trauma task force (National Child Traumatic Stress Network, 2003) presents six domains of trauma and effects:

1. Attachment v behavioural control – uncertainty about the reliability and predictability of the world.
2. Biology – communication of traumatic past events.
3. Affect regulation – difficulty planning and anticipating.
4. Dissociation acoustic and visual perceptual problems – distinct alteration in states of consciousness.
5. Cognition – difficulties in attention regulation and executive functioning.
6. Self-concept – lack of continuous predictable sense of self.

Attachment v behavioural control

Complex trauma occurs when a child experiences toxic stress over a period of time. His body prioritises survival over accessing learning and developing. Secure attachment provides a model for future productive relationships, in addition to supporting self-regulation, communication, and agency; however, the carer–child relationship can also be a source of trauma. Statistics released by the National Child Traumatic Stress Network (2003) indicate that 55–65% of the normative population demonstrate secure attachment status, and insecure attachment is apparent in 80% of maltreated children.

These indications put great emphasis on the importance of upskilling the workforce in trauma-informed practice in a context of secure and insecure attachment.

Biology

Brain development depends on the activation of genetically-based neural links which are influenced by external stimuli. The ability to maintain basic bodily functions and elementary responses to the world outside the womb are present at birth, and mature throughout the earliest period of infancy. Over time, a child develops the competence and capacity to respond to internal *and* external stimulus; however, trauma can affect the integration of left and right hemisphere brain functioning. The behaviour of children who have experienced neglect or abuse may be led by an emotional reaction with limited use of their analytical capacities. Patterns of negative and aggressive behaviour can be exhibited in the same or similar contexts, which have been referred to as schemas (National Child Traumatic Stress Network, 2003). Disruption in self-regulation affects executive functioning and attainment, and may be manifested as eating disorders, conduct disorders, or thought disorders.

A secure attachment relationship is a protective and a restorative factor in response to trauma, and encompasses the rationale of most early intervention programmes, in addition to post-traumatic stress support for adults.

Affect regulation

During the earliest stages of childhood an infant will look to the primary carer as a lens with which to view and to interpret his world. Communication, body language, perceptions, and expectations are shared with the developing baby in the context of a family and community culture. Over time the young child practices affect regulation, and acquires the skill of modulating his emotional reaction and behaviours in this context of secure attachment. Lack of positive role-modelling can result in immature emotional regulation and the potential to misinterpret circumstances, and can demonstrate inappropriate behaviours within social contexts. The many studies on adverse childhood experiences link early trauma to depression and poor prognosis of illnesses in adulthood (Felitti et al., 1998).

Dissociation, cognition, and self-concept

Dissociation is a lack of connection between cognition and emotional reaction which results in poor integration of information. There is a continuum of dissociation, and chronic trauma can be difficult to treat due to dissociation being used as a survival strategy in childhood and beyond. Adaptability, accommodation of others' needs, and the readiness to embrace new learning are all affected by dissociation. Substance misuse and self-harming commonly accompany the young person's avoidance of dealing with the primary trauma and associated issues. Ultimately development of a sense of the autobiographical self is disrupted, and may remain immature throughout the lifespan.

It is worth considering that trauma experienced by a child has a profound effect upon the parent and child. A parent may be the source of trauma, or he or she may feel intense guilt that the child could not be protected, or may deny the child's trauma which will certainly affect their attachment relationship; or perhaps the child's trauma replicates a similar situation as the one experienced by a primary carer which triggers dissociation in the parent. A child who is unsupported in the home environment may seek relationships outside the family in an attempt to alleviate the trauma effects.

Resilience can be acquired in daily living and depends on the presence of an attachment figure, not necessarily a family member, and activation of curiosity and motivation to seek out learning, to embrace knowledge, and to understand the world from a subjective *and* objective perspective. These factors contribute to the development of self, and recognition of oneself as an active agent.

Interventions which encompass four central goals are recognised as treatments which can address trauma in children and adolescents (National Child Traumatic Stress Network, 2003):

1. Feeling safe within your environment, for example, home, services, and community.
2. Development of interpersonal skills and the ability to regulate emotions.
3. Gaining comprehension of past traumatic events and reactions, and acquiring a positive attitude towards future experiences.
4. Increasing resilience and social competence.

The ability to function effectively in different social environments requires the capacity to transfer skills with or without the physical presence of an attachment figure. The skill-set is multi-layered, and includes the development of strategies to reduce reactivity to trauma prompts. These reminders of previous trauma events are usually sensory-based, for example, visual-, tactile-, sound-, smell-, or taste-orientated. The next chapter focuses upon the creation of safe, predictable environments within services and at home through professional–parent links and transition objects.

References

Bellazaire, A. 2018, 'Preventing and mitigating the effects of adverse childhood experiences', *National Conference of State Legislatures*. viewed 1 January, 2019, www.ncsl.org.

Bowlby, J. 1969, *Attachment and loss volume 1: attachment*, Pimlico, London.

Bowlby, J. 1998, *Attachment and loss volume 2: separation, anger and anxiety*, Pimlico, London.

Bretherton, I. & Munholland, K.A. 2016, 'Internal working models in attachment relationships', in J. Cassidy & P. Shaver (eds.), *Handbook of attachment theory and research*, Guilford Press, New York.

Cambridge core. 2017, *Developmental origins of early antisocial behaviour*. viewed 6 December, 2017. https://-cambridge-org.knowledge. idm.oclc.org/core/journals/development-and-.

Campbell-Barr, V., Georgeson, J. & Varga, A.N. 2015, 'Developing professional early childhood educators in England and Hungary: where has all the love gone?' *European Education*, vol. 47, no. 4, pp. 311–30. viewed 19 February, 2016. http://tandfonline.com/action/journalinformation?journalCode=meue20.

Cooper, G., Hoffman, K., Marvin, R. & Powell, B. 2000, The circle of security: Secure base and haven of security. viewed 31 May, 2016 from https://nhs.scot.knowledge.network.

Elfer, P. & Page, J. 2015, 'Pedagogy with babies: perspectives of eight nursery managers', *Early Childhood Development and Care*, vol. 185, pp. 11–12, 1762–82.

Evans, A. 2019, 'The taboo of love for children in care: its emergence through the transference relationship and in the system around the child', *Scottish Journal of Residential Child Care*, vol. 18, no. 1. viewed 1 May, 2019, www.celcis.org.uk.

Fay-Stammbach, T., Hawes, D.J. & Meredith, P. 2014, 'Parenting influences on executive function in early childhood: a review', viewed 31 December, 2017, http://onlinelibrary.wiley.com.knowledge.idm.oclc.org/doi/10.1111/cdep.12095/full.

Felitti, V.J., Anda, R.F., Nordenberg, D., Williamson, D.F., Spitz, A.M., Edwards, V., Koss, M.P. & Marks, J.S. 1998, 'Relationships of childhood abuse and household dysfunction to many of the leading causes of death in adults', *American Journal of Preventive Medicine*, vol. 14, no. 4. viewed 25 December, 2017, https://www.nhs.scot.knowledge.network.

Fonagy, P. 2003, 'Towards a developmental understanding of violence', *The British Journal of Psychiatry*, pp. 190–2. viewed 10 December, 2012, http://bjp.rcpsych.org.

Geoffroy, M.C., Côté, S.M., Borge, A.I., Larouche, F., Séguin, J.R. & Rutter, M. 2007, 'Association between nonmaternal care in the first year of life and children's receptive language skills prior to school entry: the moderating role of socio-economicstatus', *Journal of Child Psychology and Psychiatry, and Allied Disciplines*, vol. 48, no. 5, pp. 490–7. viewed 19 May, 2019, https://nhs.scot.knowledge.network.

Howes, C., Galinsky, E. & Kontos, S. 1998, 'Child care caregiver sensitivity and attachment', *Social Development*, vol. 7, no. 1, pp. 25–36. viewed 31 March, 2019, https://nhs.scot.knowledge.network.

Locke, J. 2019, *An essay concerning human understanding*, Creative Media Partners, London.

Malcolm, J. 2019, 'Services must be underpinned by love for all children', viewed 31 January, 2019, https://childreninscotland.org.uk/25-calls-respons e-services- underpinned-by-love-for-all-children/?utm_source=phplists5133 &utm_medium=emaila&.

Marvin, R., Cooper, G., Hoffman, K. & Powell, B. 2002, 'The circle of security project: attachment-based intervention with caregiver-pre-school dyads', *Attachment and Human Development*, vol. 4, no. 1, pp. 107–24. viewed 31 May, 2016, https://www.nhs.scot.knowledge.network.

Moore, T., Arefadib, N., Deery, A. & West, S. 2017, 'The first thousand days: an evidence paper', viewed 30 September, 2017, www.rch.org.au/cch.

Murray, J., Teszenyi, E., Varga, A.N., Palfi, S., Tajiyeva, M. & Iskakova, A. 2018, 'Parent-practitioner partnerships in early childhood provision in England, Hungary and Kazakhstan: similarities and differences in discourses', *Early Childhood Development and Care*, vol. 188, no. 5, pp. 594–612. viewed 1 May, 2019, http://tandfonline.com/loi/gecd20.

Nagin, D.S. & Tremblay, R. 2001, 'Parental and early childhood predictors of persistent physical aggression in boys from kindergarten to high school', *Archives of General Psychiatry*, vol. 58, no. 4. viewed 12 June, 2012, http://archpsyc.jamenetwork.com/.

National Child Traumatic Stress Network (NCTSN). 2003, 'Complex trauma in children and adolescents', viewed 1 May, 2019, https://nctsn.org/resources/co mplex-trauma-children-and-adolescents.

Pauen, S. & Early Development of Self-Regulation Group (EDOS). 2016, 'Understanding early development of self-regulation and co-regulation: EDOS and Process of Self and Co-Regulation (PROSECO)', *Journal of Self-Regulation and Regulation*, vol. 2. viewed 31 December, 2017 www.nhs.scot.knowledge. network.

Pote, I., Doubell, L., Brims, L., Larbie, J., Stock, L. & Lewing, B. 2019, *Engaging disadvantaged and vulnerable parents, an evidence review*, Early Intervention Foundation, London.

Schore, A.N. 2015, 'Review of the emotional life of your brain', *Psychoanalytic Psychology*, vol. 32, no. 3, pp. 539–47.

Shirvanian, N. & Michael, T. 2017, 'Implementation of attachment theory into early childhood settings', *The International Education Journal: Comparative Perspectives*, vol. 16, no. 2, pp. 97–115. viewed 1 January, 2019 from, https://op enjournals.library.sydney.edu.au/index.php/IEJ.

Tizard, B. 2009, 'Looking back: the making and breaking of attachment theory', *The British Psychological Society*, vol. 22, pp. 902–3. British Psychological Society, London.

Turner, M., Beckwith, H., Duschinsky, R., Forslund, T., Foster, S.L., Coughlan, B., Pal, S. & Schuengel, C. 2019, 'Attachment difficulties and disorders', viewed 25 May, 2019, https://nhs.scot.knowledge.network.

Van der Kolk, B. 2003, 'The neurobiology of childhood trauma and abuse', *Child and Adolescent Psychiatric Clinics of North America*, viewed 17 May, 2016, https://www.researchgate.net/publication/10779024.
Whitters, H.G. 2017, *Nursery nurse to early years' practitioner: role, relationships and responsibilities*, Routledge, Abingdon.
Whitters, H.G. 2018, *Family learning to inclusion: theory, practice, and partnerships*, Routledge, Abingdon.
Whitters, H.G. 2019, *Attainment and executive functioning in the early years: research and inclusive practice for lifelong learning*, Routledge, Abingdon.

3 Learning environments in the earliest years

It is easy to create a stimulating learning environment for children in their earliest years. It is easy to adhere to curricular guidance by presenting opportunities for child-led play. It is also easy to meet health and safety requirements within an early years service; however, an implementation gap can arise between the environment and a child's ability and capacity to access knowledge, to gain understanding, and to increase his or her executive functioning. This chapter presents research and comprehension of learning from the external perspective of an educational arena, in addition to internal processes which contribute to the child's agency.

Example from practice

Tong stood on the periphery of his learning environment – the low sunshine created lines of dappled shadows on the sanded floorboards. A light breeze gently swayed the branches of trees which flanked the outside path. Rectangular desks had been placed to form stations around the room, two by two, and four by four, as receptacles for the lessons of the day. There were red and blue boxes with the lids tantalisingly ajar, packs of new felt-pens with the colours lined side by side, waiting to be chosen, chunky wooden jigsaws still covered in clear packaging, and mysterious objects making odd shapes within linen re-cycling bags. The school classroom was ready and waiting for Tong and his five-year-old peers to enter, ready for "Golden Time." It was Friday afternoon in the local primary school, and the period for young learners to relax after a busy week.

However, Tong's thoughts were elsewhere. Friday afternoon Golden Time signalled a forthcoming transition and the young boy was acutely aware that the weekend break lay ahead. Two days of home-time, and childhood adversities. Tong had a twin sister, Rita-Li, who had a terminal illness. This little girl would spend weekdays in hospital but on

Saturdays and Sundays come home. Tong loved his sister dearly but five years of age was too young to understand why his mother would clean the house and move furniture on a Friday night, why relatives visited Rita-Li every weekend and brought her presents, why his twin could sleep in the favoured spot beside his mother, why he had to play quietly in the bedroom by himself; in short, he was too young to comprehend the effects of this adversity upon his mother, father, aunts, uncles, grandparents, and himself.

Childhood adversities, and the resultant toxic stress, cannot always be categorised into the common sources as recognised in research (Scottish Government, 2018). Negative effects during the formative years of children can also occur through illness of kith and kin. Most parents will naturally incline their care and emotions towards a child who is sick, and inadvertently bypass the needs of siblings who are suffering in silence. Emotional stresses invade the young Tong's wellbeing – anger, fear, confusion, rejection. Every family experiences adversities, and this chapter focuses upon the creation of nurturing environments in response to each child's interpretation, and emotional reactions, as opposed to stereotypical assumptions which are informed by the source of adversity. Nitecki and Chung (2016) describe the theoretical implications of "place-based education" as the environment in which play occurs *and* the child's internal reactions to play.

Our first learning environment

The embryo is formed at conception, and genetic material from egg and sperm combine; therefore a set of genes is created which reflects the environmental exposures of both parents prior to parenthood. Moore et al. (2017) vividly describe the embryo's responses to signals from the mother's reproductive tract through changes in embryonic fluid in accordance with the mother's nutritional, metabolic, and inflammatory states. Over many decades promotion of the mother's health in the pre- and peri-conception periods has been the practical response from governments throughout the world to maintain a healthy and fit population.

Developmental plasticity of the embryo is prime at this stage, and influenced directly by the environmental cues of the surrounding fluid. **Developmental plasticity** is a current term which is used to describe the human ability to adapt to different social and physical environments in order to maintain, or to increase, operational skills. **Neuroplasticity** refers to the biological capacity of the central nervous system to alter the brain architecture as a response to internal and external influences. Adaptation can support or hinder development as direct and indirect exposure to experiences can lead to positive and negative consequences.

Epigenetics

Epigenetic change is often described as interaction between genes and the environment which influences the way in which genes function but which does not change them per se (Moore et al., 2017). These processes are complex but clearly represent an approach to maximising survival within a particular, external environment post-birth. The potential for the embryo to be put at risk is high within the context of families who live in adversity. Family adversities can affect an embryo through poor health of the mother during pregnancy and/or through the negative effects from the gene pool of the mother or father which commence at conception, and continue thereafter. Ahead is a lifetime of epigenetic changes and effects which increase or decrease executive functioning.

Moore (2015) explains the term **genome** as an organism's entire set of DNA, and describes the genome as developing throughout the life-span as opposed to being fixed at birth. The inter-generational impact of adversity has been communicated more widely within academia and practice in recent years due to an increase in understanding from sociology, neuroscience, childcare and education, and many other fields related to human development. Genes may remain dormant throughout life until the necessary conditions are experienced. Our understanding of childhood adversities is greater than before, and it is known that personality is also a factor in epigenetic change. Experiences may be significant to one person, and not to another, despite similar gene potential.

The first 1,000 days of life are regarded as a sensitive period for critical epigenetic changes although brain plasticity remains throughout our life-span to a lesser degree. It is interesting that epigenetic changes are linked to many physical *or* cognitive disorders, for example, cardiovascular disease and autistic spectrum disorder (Ismail et al., 2017). These findings present the route to intervention as each child's interplay with the learning environment can be supported by practitioners or primary carers. This knowledge and understanding of gene potential highlights the importance of focusing upon the implementation gap between presentation of educational experiences, and the realisation of learning which occurs within each child.

Negative effects which were experienced by parents and grandparents can be transmitted across generations, and result in **non-genomic** transmission of disease (Champagne, 2015). This means that children inherit genes which are already in a state of activation due to the experiences of their predecessors which increases the potential for adverse effects.

Moore et al. (2017) use the term **social determinants** to describe the social, economic, and environmental conditions which influence health and wellbeing. Parental trauma, and the resultant insecure attachment with a child, is often cited as a source of inter-generational adversity. Poverty is also a common influence which can impose toxic stress upon a family, and it is one example which is understood, and responded to, by the general public. Issues associated with poverty are often highlighted in the media in a context of local responses in the form of food banks and charity donations within a community.

New adversities also come to the fore with each generation: for example, Australia records allergic reactions as prevalent in the current generation of children but rarely exhibited by their parents or grandparents. This continent has one of the highest rates of allergic diseases in the world. During the last ten years there has been a reported five-fold increase in anaphylaxis in pre-school children in Australia (Moore et al., 2017).

Bernier et al. (2012) describe influences from social and environmental conditions upon two behavioural systems: attachment and exploratory. These systems of human development are complimentary in the context of a secure attachment relationship. Findings from this research indicate a direct link between impulse control at three years of age, attachment, and parenting style. The three classic parenting styles are identified by Zarra-Nezhad et al. (2014) as affectionate, controlling behaviour, and psychological control. I find that parents tend to describe a combination of these styles which is situation-dependent, although adversity as experienced by an adult can result in the dominant use of one style. The key to change is supporting parents in understanding the effect of parenting styles upon children, and in using the creation of secure attachment as the optimum foundation for attainment.

Example from practice

Evan is three years old. He is a little boy who engages well with learning. Evan's blond curls bob up and down, and his hands and feet are always wriggling as we interact. He avidly seeks out more and more knowledge of his world. Evan's older sister, Cerys, has been diagnosed with autistic spectrum disorder and attention deficit hyperactivity disorder. Mum and Dad are worried...

Is Evan showing early signs of the same conditions? Is Evan simply copying his sister's reactions? Can Evan be supported? Can nursery help?

Mum, Dad, and Evan join our Family Learning Project: play sessions for extended families to learn about each other's strengths and areas for development; a medium of learning in which mothers and fathers gain confidence and feel pride, pride in Evan's achievements and pride in their development of parenting skills.

Specific toys encourage reciprocity between adult and child, and ignite curiosity for exploration, for questioning, for forming opinions, and for challenging the views of others. Challenges lead to greater understanding, as well as the ability to transfer knowledge and apply it to a multitude of circumstances in the daily interactions with our world.

Introductory session

The mother and father sit close together on the checked red settee in the family centre. I notice that Dad is perched on the edge of a cushion as if preparing for flight. Mum demonstrates anxiety as she twists the dark brown leather strap of her shoulder-bag.

I smile and thank the couple for attending. I commence the session: "What would you like to change today?" Parents or any primary carers always know what they don't know!

As human beings we often focus upon our negative output, and feel reticent about acknowledging our skills. All parents have an emotive issue to solve which takes priority over any general parenting strategies which a facilitator may be keen to share. The initial stage should focus upon development of an effective professional–parent working partnership, and embrace the prioritising of support which is presented by parents regarding their needs. I strive to achieve the latest publicised practice guidelines in delivering interventions to couples: support retention, promote accessibility for each couple's needs, adapt and personalise content and delivery, and finally create the "therapeutic alliance" (Pote et al., 2019).

Dad quickly responds to the question with a plea for help: "Evan won't hold hands." I notice from the short construction of this comment that Evan's father has low expectations of himself and his child. I ask for a recent example. Encouraging parents to describe incidents which have just taken place contributes in many ways to effective facilitation. Asking pertinent questions to increase the details shared, and to expose the accompanying emotion, provides a valuable foundation for supporting the development of parenting skills. For example:

Dad: "As we got out of the car I was worried that Evan would run away while I was locking the doors so I used an angry voice to try and keep him beside me. Then I had to give him a row because he crouched down beside another car in your car-park. Everyone was watching out of the café window. I don't know what to do any more."

Within a few moments I had been given a summary of this father's interpretation, and perception, of his parenting skills and his son's behaviour. Sharing the story had given me a base of knowledge and understanding of the family:

- The father was aware of environmental health and safety for his three-year-old son.
- The daily practical circumstances which surround the family lifestyle.
- The father's personal and public perception of his parenting skills.
- The father's motivation to change and to support his son.

Transitions

By using this evocative example Evan's father had inadvertently highlighted a significant aspect of children's learning and development – **transitions**. Already I had a context for parenting to use in the creation of implicit memories, in addition to explicit memories, and to promote the application of knowledge beyond the confines of the formal intervention. Research has indicated that home learning may involve parents, extended family, or siblings (Hunt et al., 2011). Parents who are participating in a family programme within a service will represent the knowledge to their family, and it is essential that these primary carers understand their actions, and increase in parenting skills.

Effective transitions are an integral component of the composite of learning. Multiple "home" environments for children are common due to a variety of circumstances which encompass daily family life. For example, many parents are estranged, and consequently shared-care arrangements emerge for the children: some children have temporary homes within short-term respite care, or longer-term foster-care. Many families have access to support from relatives, kinship carers, or others, and informal arrangements result in periods of childhood out-with the birth-family home. An environment may be superb with regard to stimulation for children but if a child has not coped well with the transition from his or her previous circumstance then involvement, wellbeing, and executive functioning will undoubtedly be affected. Holding hands with a parent creates an attachment-transition which will support Evan in maintaining his capacity and ability to learn within different contexts. The little boy's neural networks will connect his actions, task-shifting, operational skills, and most importantly emotional reaction which form his executive functioning. The baseline of resilience for potential lifetime effect is forming in the earliest years of childhood.

Fifty years ago Winnicott (1971) used the term **transitional phenomena** to indicate this transference of the child's wellbeing and potential achievement between environments. Winnicott referred to the symbolism associated with transitions for each child, and she recognised that the physical presence of a parent could be representative of a transition object. Over time presence will be replaced by symbolic representation which is informed by implicit memories, and associated with coping strategies, personal to each child or adult.

Strategies

I nod to Evan's parents, add a few words of acknowledgement and empathy regarding the father's recounting of his stressful experience this morning, and present practical strategies followed by explanation:

- Focus upon transitions, for example, leaving the car and entering a service, leaving the house to go to nursery, leaving the supermarket to return home.

  Transitions are difficult for all children, and occur frequently throughout each day. Supporting transitions is a major achievement by a parent which facilitates the child's capacity to learn.
- Practise in the safety of the home environment.

  Minimise external difficulties, for example, the pressure of a public audience watching your actions. Choose an opportunity to practise promoting positive behaviour in which there are not restrictions of time. A home environment provides multiple circumstances in which to practise hand-holding with a child, for example, on the way to the bathroom to have a bath in the morning, taking the rubbish out to your re-cycling bin, hanging out the washing.
- Bend down, give eye contact.

  This is a classic parenting skill to engage your child and gain attention for learning.
- Offer your hand to Evan as opposed to taking his hand, and say, "Evan, hand please!"

  This is a significant strategy which can support a child's self-regulation by giving him a choice, offering "thinking time" for the child to make a decision, and promoting self-regulation of behaviour. Auditory and visual prompting reinforces the social boundary by creating explicit memories of expectations and patterns of behaviour. Positivity from the parent nurtures an implicit memory based upon the "feel-good" factor.

- Give two clear choices in a matter of fact voice, for example, "Evan, you can choose to take my hand and we will go to nursery and play or you can choose to stand here."

This is a set of circumstances and consequences, not punishment, which are easily understood and adhered to. Descriptive praise and acknowledgement of the child making a good social choice influences the implicit memories which are activated on the next similar occasion.

Evan's mother quickly indicates her stance and interrupts: "Evan won't take hands. Evan will slide on a heap on the floor or run away to hide under the hall table." This maternal insight is useful as it gives me an understanding that Evan and his mother have developed patterns of behaviour.

Responses have got to be simple and practical. Promotion of positive behaviour is accumulative, and occurs exponentially:

- Return Evan to the transition point at the front door, and repeat the choices.
- Be prepared to wait, to watch, to understand your child, and to welcome good choice-making.
- Do not adopt Evan's emotions – containment is key.
- Children learn rapidly with appropriate emotional support.

Evan is bored with listening to the adults talking. He dances sideways towards the door, and observes me carefully. Evan attempts to swing on the broad silver metal handle – positioned perfectly at child-height. I grasp the opportunity, and say to Dad, "Take Evan into the cloakroom to collect his slippers and share the plan, and ask him to take your hand before you leave the room and walk up the corridor."

The scene plays out: Dad promotes the hand-holding strategy, and Evan predictably slumps to the floor. Boundary is repeated staccato-like but affirmatively by Dad, and Evan stamps his foot, then pauses. Suddenly the little boy thrusts his hand into his father's outstretched palm, and father and son are conjoined! Spontaneously Dad ruffles Evan's blond curls, and grins. The application of social boundaries should not disempower a child or parent but present realistic and achievable goals.

It is well-known that children will often make positive behavioural choices in response to parents in the presence of a familiar professional in a service. Environments and people represent prompts to children which activate the neural networks to link actions and consequences. Supporting primary carers to change their parenting styles is challenging for the service-provider but merging theory and practice in situ can instil confidence and activate latent skills in parents.

Cultural sensitivity

As professionals we need to have a well-prepared agenda which includes areas for development, projected outcomes, and possible routes for intervention; however, as human beings we need to respond to another's needs in order to recognise the emotional status of a parent, and thereafter to tailor our delivery of knowledge and practical skills in accordance with the primary carer's ability and capacity to learn at a particular moment in time. Effective and valid teaching is not simply presenting knowledge, but the creation of a medium which supports understanding – relationship-based practice.

A professional will have a checklist of information to share with a parent in a context of implementing formal support. We are required to justify the time spent on delivering interventions which may be packaged neatly within inflexible guidelines. Through years of presenting formal and informal programmes, I have gained a deep understanding of the importance of "teaching," **and** "observing how others are learning," and consequently adjusting my pre-conceived plan.

Planned lessons are necessary in the implementation, and auditing, of structured parenting programmes but a weakness can occur if the facilitator does not notice each of the participants uptake of knowledge and adapt accordingly. Adaptation should not incur changes to the integrity or validity of formal programmes but may encompass different communication strategies, for example, explanation of technical terms to suit the culture of recipients, or interacting at a slower pace, or perhaps introducing frequent comfort breaks or shortening the sessions. Parents' examples can also be used as exemplars to illustrate learning as opposed to generic coursework scenarios. **Cultural sensitivity** is a term applied by Moran et al. (2004) to describe this phenomenon.

I feel that the joy of teaching is experienced by witnessing an increase in comprehension, and in application of knowledge by others which often leads to re-configuration of the inner working model. Any professional in a teaching role should always be learning from participants, whether adults or children. It is important to recognise achievement by parents and to ask, "How do you feel?" This approach supports the creation of implicit memories by associating emotion and actions.

Facilitating a programme requires understanding the rationale by reviewing the research, considering the evaluations, relating to national issues and curricula, adapting delivery to local culture if applicable, and believing in the strategies of intervention. Belief of a facilitator is essential to positive outcomes – belief in the programme, and a communicable belief that the primary carer can achieve.

Residential care

Furnivall (2011) discusses emotional transition difficulties in an extreme context for children who are looked after in residential or foster care, and emphasises the importance of attachment-transitions as key workers change. The key worker, as an attachment figure in a professional context, cannot be available for children on a long-term basis. Shift patterns of working, annual leave, sick leave, and career progression are all circumstances in which the key worker may be absent or indeed the role may have to be reallocated to another person.

Furnivall's research indicates the importance of transitory objects as reminders of an attachment relationship which provides scope for the principles of trust and honesty to be maintained, and re-created with another key person. This author suggests celebrating transitions as a strategy to prepare a child for change in attachment figure; however, transitions can occur unexpectedly and rapidly in response to a crisis which can be detrimental to a child who has already experienced trauma in the birth family. The timescale of a child being in residential or foster care is always indeterminate, and usually depends on progress by parents in developing skills and ability to care for their children. Furnivall recommends that key workers and a care environment should continue to offer a secure base to every child or young person who has experienced a transition away from the service. This provides a challenge for strategic and practical planners.

Research by Robinson and Brown (2016) investigated potential links between the emotional impact of transitions and the physical environment of daily living in a context of residential care. The authors focus upon sensory processing and the link to environmental cues within a setting. An increase in sensory awareness can result in environmental features and trauma merging together in the form of explicit memories. Associative implicit memories, which these authors described as automatic and unconscious, are also formed and prompt external actions and emotional reaction. This research is informative to practice and clearly expands the knowledge of environmental impact and the internal working mechanisms of children, young people, and adults who experience post-traumatic stress.

Findings indicate that trauma which occurs during an infant's *pre-verbal stage* will be processed at a sensory level, and this can result in extreme emotional reaction without an infant having the capacity to make sense of the experience. "Fragmented memories" is a term applied by Robinson and Brown (2016). Instinctive strategies of fight, flight, or freeze may be the child's predominant response to fragmented memories which are closely associated with trauma.

Learning environment

Choice of setting

Gur (2014) investigated the physical structures of early years settings in Turkey by accessing a sample set of 95 parents and professionals. The transition points were particularly significant in supporting children in moving positively from the culture of the home environment, transposed by the presence of their parents, into the organisational culture of the early years setting. A covered interim entry station was regarded as important, for example a roofed porch area to provide shelter and a welcome break from inclement weather, and/or a cloakroom space with adult and child seating.

Parents expressed that clarity in identifying the entrance was essential to promote ease of admission but also positivity to their children. An inability to find the way into a building can quickly provoke anxiety in an adult which is easily transferred to a child who may already be sensing a forthcoming stressful separation from a primary carer. Visual prompts in the form of windows at child-level provided the maximum opportunity for new children to observe peers at play, and to gain an understanding of the purpose of the building as they approached the entrance.

Visibility in the local community, and easy transporting, was also attractive to parents in addition to familiarity with a building, prior to attendance. The ability to walk to the service from home was expressed by parents as conducive to a positive transition, and provided time for children and parents to be prepared, to recall prior experiences, and to focus upon "what happens next." Outdoor green play areas and access to local natural environment in the community were additional selection criteria described by parents and practitioners.

Surprisingly, recommendation of a service was not highlighted in this research (Gur, 2014). As a long-standing practitioner in a community setting I have found that this selection criteria is often expressed as the main reason for referral to the service by parents, and multi-agency professionals. Relationship-based practice is important, regardless of the physical structure of a building, and often reflects family links to staff members over many years, or previous professional partnerships.

Indoors

An optimum learning environment should respond to explicit and implicit influences on children. The environmental checklist for autistic spectrum disorders (Simpson, 2009) is used by some professionals as an assessment tool in order to optimise opportunities for learning. The checklist is completed in relation to the general environment, and the rationale is to maximise learning by reducing excessive stimulation which is imposed through sensory input. Interestingly the checklist has been compiled and presented as a positive practice model by asking the reader pertinent questions in the context of a deficit model, for example, "Is the background cluttered with furniture?"

Presentation of knowledge in checklists can lead learners towards comprehension but may also invoke misinterpretation. Setting an environment by following a generic checklist is not effective practice, and does not support personalisation of a learning arena for the individual child. Each point on a checklist contains knowledge and implies application of information. Implementation should always be preceded by rigorous discussion between practitioners in order to gain clarity of the rationale. Knowledge is necessary but understanding is key to continuous professional development.

An example can be gained by dissection of one question from the aforementioned checklist (Simpson, 2009): "Is the background cluttered with furniture?" provides layers of information which need to be extracted and interpreted for practice:

- The question implies that a background context has a potentially negative effect upon a child's learning within her proximal environment – practitioners need to consider why and how peripheral items impact.
- The term "cluttered" implies chaos and distraction through the presence of furniture – practitioners need to consider how these features are assessed, and the effect upon learning.
- Implication that the furniture is additional to the main focus of learning – practitioners need to consider if the furniture is actually surplus to learning requirements or complimentary to the knowledge which is being shared.

Furniture can often represent the culture and identity of a service. Research has indicated the important message which is communicated to learners by the place in which education occurs. The constructivist approach relates to experiences accumulated from the environs which impact upon the internal reactions of each child (Nitecki & Chung, 2016).

I have found that guidance is most useful if it is presented as a positive model of practice.

Example from practice

Children's choice area

This area should support children in achieving their highest level of involvement and attainment in addition to a secure attachment relationship with an adult which incurs a high level of wellbeing.

Rajina is two and a half years old and her current interests lie within the children's choice area. Key workers have recently moved the open-shelved cupboard to ensure that distractions from traffic of children, adults, or other external influences are minimised. A student sits quietly on one side, without interrupting but ready to participate, and to scaffold Rajina's play as required. Each choice has a particular container. Choices are visible to attract the little girl's attention but presented with challenges for problem-solvers: screw-top lids, snap-on lids, chunky zips, large buttons, sticky tape, or drawstrings. Rajina's prowess is stretched, and her high- and low-level functioning evolves through problem-solving. Adjoining choices give prompts, links to concepts, or simply ideas to extend creativity and imagination, and to impose order upon the play experience by facilitating tidy-up time!

Snack and tooth-brushing area

This area should support children in developing self-help skills, making social and personal choices to understand links between hunger/ thirst/food and drink, balancing and sitting safely, using fine motor skills, and communicating verbally or using body language/prompts. The area should also support children in waiting patiently in turn-taking, anticipating routines, copying peers and adults, and nurturing the attachment relationship with a key worker.

Bartosz loves food! His mother has recorded this main interest for her son on his nursery application form. The four-year-old has settled quickly into the routines, and gained an ability to recognise the cues which precede the advent of snack. Key workers have not needed to support Bartosz as his chosen role of helper has given him pride, a sense of order, and the realisation of his desired outcome – fruit, milk, or water, and the healthy snack of the day.

Cleaning tables to achieve a shiny glow, counting chairs, and sorting colours of plates with companion cups provide rich learning experiences in this area, in addition to promotion of citizenship, and care for the environment. Matching toothbrushes to their owners is a task designated to key workers but the young Bartosz watches and learns, and today he is remembering and confidently shouting out each child's name in relation to the pictures of animals which adorn the toothbrush receptacle – a red and blue bus which gives each child's brush a special holder identified by name and a picture of an animal. Everyday routines present stimulating and extensive learning opportunities.

Arts and crafts/creative imaginative play – home play and small world play.

These areas should allow free expression of play by each child at low and high levels, and facilitate creation of secure attachment relationships with adults, and friendships with peers.

Nuahua is a petite five-year-old – a pre-schooler who is gradually outgrowing the nursery experience, and seeking more challenges to quench a desire for knowledge and understanding of her world. Home play and small world artefacts provide an outlet for her needs, as Nuahua's imagination is vivid, and influenced by her many interests. Parallel play and cooperative play are open routes for this little girl to choose alongside solitary play or participation with peers in response to her capacity, and desire to socialise at a point in time.

Floor play and table-top areas

These areas should support children in using comfortable, safe learning positions in order to use two hands in play, and in increasing eye–hand coordination. They should present opportunities to mix resources, to problem-solve, and to extend knowledge and skill over time, in a context of secure attachment and supportive scaffolding of play by adults.

"Dimiro is going to be an engineer," says his father proudly at the induction session to nursery. Hopes and dreams of parents are important and support attainment in children and families through belief in success and fulfilment, whatever the chosen outcome. Table-top activities and floor play are positioned carefully side by side, and toys have become transferrable between them, as implemented by Dimiro's decision-making. His daily creations are based upon family experiences, and observations in the community. Today, the four-year-old is standing tall to achieve a black and white tower, reminiscent of the flats which are being constructed beside the local post office. This activity is supporting Dimiro in using his memory and in consolidating his learning.

Book corner and physical play

These areas should provide a contrast to children regarding up-regulation and down-regulation, in addition to opportunities for independent play, peer-play, and adult-supported play.

Musa and Hassan, two brothers who attend nursery, play together, and learn together about their extended world. The physical play and book corner are juxtaposed in this setting, providing activity or rest. One area promotes the use of equipment, to gain balance, to understand speed, height, and safety, and to extend gross motor skills. Equally important is the outcome from promoting Musa's and Hassan's understanding of their physical selves, without equipment – spatial awareness and proprioception. The brothers communicate instinctively, often silently, and access the book corner as one. Recognising your need to down-regulate, to re-generate energy, and thereafter to re-convene your play, are essential life-skills.

Outdoors

Research (Robinson & Brown, 2016) refers to the use of outdoor spaces to induce a calm and ambient atmosphere. Regular access to the outdoor environment is currently promoted throughout many countries as a response to the mental health crisis which is encompassing the children and young people of today. Outdoor exercise was termed "green exercise" by Barton and Pretty (2010) within research upon adults which used a comparative study to investigate short- and long-term health benefits. The researchers linked the use of outdoor environment as a significant contribution to health of the population. The findings indicated that self-esteem and mood improved through exposure to green environments with an increase in positive effects from the presence of water. There was not a marked difference in the self-esteem between genders but the greatest change was demonstrated by the youngest participants, and participants who had existing mental health conditions.

Interaction with the natural world is explored by Louv (2005) as an intervention which promotes good health in addition to offering leisure pursuits. This researcher applies a descriptor "nature deficit disorder" to indicate the negative effects which relate to lack of access to outdoor stimulation in the specific context of urban dwelling.

Wilson (1997) reviews the topic from a different perspective, and she suggests that **environmental sensitivity** can be nurtured through the provision of outdoor play opportunities. Outcomes for the child mirror the outcomes for nature. For example, the child's understanding of himself as relevant, respected, and looked after by society is gained through his comprehension and response to the natural world.

Outdoor nurseries have expanded in many countries throughout the world in the last decade, and provide safe "outdoor-classrooms" for parents, children, and practitioners. The benefits of this type of play were formally recognised through ideas and principles promoted as Forest Schools in the United Kingdom, in the late 1990s. The model of learning represented the well-established Nordic implementation of education over the last 100 years (O'Brien & Murray, 2007).

Example from practice

A common purchase in early years settings is a butterfly farm. For a small cost a butterfly pack with net, caterpillars, and pictorial instructions can be delivered directly to a nursery. Kenneth and Ailidh are friends, best friends. The earliest relationships between peers are significant in providing a blue-print of the joy of cooperating with another, the thrill of laughing and sharing, and the impact of responding to each other's emotions.

Kenneth confidently plunges his hand into the butterfly net and picks up a small slice of orange. A developing blue and white butterfly flaps her new wings slowly as her temporary resting place is moved. She raises antennae to test the environment and detects the presence of the two excited children. Kenneth urges Ailidh to touch the insect. He smiles, and reassures his friend by nodding furiously as she tentatively stretches her little finger towards the butterfly.

This activity creates a stimulating opportunity for young children to learn about nurturing the environment, to incite curiosity about growth, to create links between food, water, shelter, and health, and to consider the wonder of our natural world through the release of mature butterflies into an urban environment. "Gentle touching" is the cry from practitioners as little two-year-old fingers attempt to grasp the fluttering insects. Role-modelling sensitive responding from adult to child encourages replication from child to developing butterflies, and ultimately the promotion of environmental sensitivity.

Provision of outdoor play

Outdoor play at the beginning, and throughout, each session has become a norm in United Kingdom early years educational settings. Most children currently have part-time placements although this circumstance is rapidly changing as an increase in funding in the early years sector is enabling parents to resume full-time employment soon after childbirth.

There has been a recent increase in government-funded childcare hours in Scotland to 600 hours per year, for each child aged 3–5 years, with a proposal of 1,140 hours per year by 2020. It is proposed that outdoor provision can respond to three areas of need in Scotland: intervention in the earliest years of childhood, an increase in the health and wellbeing of communities, and innovative venues to fulfil provision of extended childcare and education.

Additionally, the Scottish Government implemented funding termed "Eligible 2s" in 2017 in order to support vulnerable families in accessing services. The criteria relates to families who are deemed to live in poverty, and many beneficiaries are supported by social work on a voluntary basis. The Royal College of Paediatrics and Child Health (2019), in Scotland, forecast that three key policies of addressing poverty, obesity, and mental health will respond positively to reducing the current statistic of 450 deaths of infants, children, and young people in Scotland per year.

Glucose

Glucose is identified as a contributing factor to an increase in wellbeing, directed attention, and consequently executive functioning. The effect is most apparent for children who are fatigued, and participating in tasks which are complex as opposed to familiar daily routines (Kaplan & Berman, 2010).

If glucose is replenished to the required level for the individual then self-regulation can be improved, and there is a positive impact upon social and interpersonal interactions (Gailliot & Baumeister, 2007). A current practical example can be taken from the context of outdoor nurseries. A common expectation of outdoor settings is the child's increase in awareness of hunger and thirst, and subsequent link to good health and a feeling of wellbeing. Outcomes which are sought from an outdoor-based implementation of the curriculum are the child's ability to seek support from adults, to access her own packed lunch and water bottle as required, and to identify a need for rest at appropriate times. These achievements are essential to each child gaining comprehension of her sense of self, and managing her own physical body and emotional wellbeing, in order to maintain and to increase operational skills in different environments.

Example from practice

> *Children who attend morning sessions tend to embrace the outdoor play experience with motivation, great physical energy, and a desire to seek out learning. The youngest afternoon attenders are invariably tired from morning activities at home, or outside, and may favour sedentary activities albeit in a natural environment.*
>
> *Ayyan is an afternoon boy and attends his nursery on a regular basis. This three-year-old learner is tired today, and seeks out the shade of a blossoming apple tree in the nursery garden. Ayyan's mother shrugs resignedly as she explains that the family sleep patterns are disturbed by his new baby sister, and tiredness has become the norm. However, a child's physical wellbeing and motivation to seek out adventures is easily refreshed with food, drink, and a short break under the leafy green branches.*

Daytime rest for nursery children always incorporates a semblance of learning which encourages intrepid explorers to relax, and to re-generate energy for the next chapter of play. Ayyan sits on a purple tartan picnic-rug, and eats a snack as he watches two little spiders climbing over and under the ferns which surrounded the old fruit tree. The spiders are challenged by the curly green fronds of the plants which encapsulate their fragile legs, and Ayyan is absorbed by the spectacle. Ten minutes later he jumps up, and skips across the soft damp grass to greet his peers.

The daily timetable for early years, and primary, reflects the comprehension of childcare and education practitioners that outdoor activity, and deep level learning, are complimentary aspects of children's development. A pattern of outdoor experiences, rest, and nurture, and a variety of activities, should be established for each setting and individual children.

Attention restoration theory and practice

Ohly et al. (2016) explain this phenomenon in the context of **Attention Restoration Theory**. These authors reviewed 31 studies which investigated attention fatigue: a condition associated with low self-regulation, poor decision-making, and physical ill-health. The findings indicated that ability and capacity to concentrate, and ultimately to achieve an increase in executive functioning, can be restored through exposure to natural environments. The exact aspect of attention focus which was affected positively by the natural context was not identified in this review but ongoing research is exploring the issue.

Attention restoration theory explains the ability and capacity to re-focus and increase attention to learning in four categories (Kaplan, 1995). The outcome is improved self-regulation and executive functioning:

1. Release from daily adversities.
2. Exposure to wide spaces and broader contexts of living.
3. Opportunities to follow personal interests leading to enhanced motivation to learn.
4. Experiencing new and undemanding stimuli.

The principles of fascination, compatibility, and extension traverse the four categories as described by Kaplan (1995). Fascination implies time for reflection; however, Kaplan made an important distinction between "hard fascination," for example watching a sporting game, or "soft fascination" which occurs within the natural environment, for example, observing a bumble-bee crawling upon a flower.

Hard fascination activities tend to have identifiable goals, and include positive expectations and perceptions which may have been influenced by prior experiences, or the attitude of fellow participators. An outcome of hard fascination is an increase in stimulation of the human senses which may incur a physiological reaction such as rapid heart-beat and a feeling of anxiety. Alternatively, **soft fascination** activities may not have a goal which is known, or is important, to the observer. An outcome of soft fascination is reflection which may incur a restorative effect upon the human body, and an increase in awareness of self and the wonder of nature.

A further study by Kaplan and Berman (2010) identified the natural environment as a source with which to gain restoration of these capacities. Explanation promotes two types of attention: voluntary or involuntary. Voluntary attention or the updated term of **directed attention** requires a human being to consciously focus upon an activity. **Involuntary attention** requires less effort due to a specific interest of the individual being met or attraction to the content through curiosity or prior experiences. The outdoor environment is commonly regarded as a context in which children and adults demonstrate involuntary attention; however, the restoration effect also supports the use of directed attention.

Many people will enter the outdoor arena with a pre-conceived plan which may be time-limited or context-dependent, for example traversing a specific hill, walking in a circuit round a park, sun-bathing in the back garden, or interacting with water. Fulfilment of these ideas can increase the compatibility of the individual with nature, increase the ameliorative effects, and reduce attention-fatigue.

Attention deficit hyperactivity disorder

Good health *and* attainment were linked by Kuo and Taylor (2004) in an interesting study upon play within green spaces, and the use of pictures and slides of the natural world. The research focused upon children who had been diagnosed with attention deficit hyperactivity disorder (ADHD). The authors indicated that symptoms associated with **attention-fatigue**, which is a periodic condition, were similar to characteristics of ADHD, which is a long-term condition. Interaction with green experiences was linked to an increase in attainment regarding school work which immediately succeeded active outdoor play, or following exposure to pictorial representation of outdoor experiences. The findings concluded that exercise in green spaces reduced the characteristic of attention-fatigue, and increased capacity for learning.

Structural environments

The physical structure of play environments is often constructed in response to the development of gross motor skills. McLoyd (1983) investigated structure and imaginative play, and the study promotes the importance of learning artefacts being presented at high and low structural levels. The findings indicated that a high structure resulted in an increase in associated pretend play by children as individuals, but did not significantly affect cooperative play in sample sets of children aged 3–5 years. Collado and Staats (2016) recently conducted a review of green vegetation in outdoor learning environments, and found a link between greater concentration in pre-school children and settings which offered high and low areas of natural vegetation for play.

It is important for practitioners in each setting to observe children at play, and to analyse the characteristics which aid attention restoration, in addition to potential barriers, within the cultural context of the area and group of service-users. Additionally, feedback from the children and parents, as service-users, is essential in the development of any play spaces indoors and outdoors. An example of direct feedback from children is the data of 175 participants which was collated in a study by Corraliza et al. (2012). The results indicated that children who were exposed to nature on a regular basis had increased coping strategies in response to adversities. Interestingly the children who were most vulnerable experienced the greatest positive effects from contact with the natural environment.

Outdoors to indoors

The therapeutic value of natural spaces is induced by a combination of factors, and architects have been attempting to reproduce this restorative ambience internally over many years. The colour green has long been recognised as blending easily with other colours on a visual level, and education services often display information on a green background frieze.

New hospitals in the United Kingdom and elsewhere have representations of the outdoors through large murals in waiting areas which depict green trees and woodland paths. This projection of nature attracts attention and directs a patient's focus forward and beyond into the distance, on an imaginative journey. Previous authors have identified positive benefits from simply looking at green views internally or externally without practical interaction (Barton & Pretty, 2010; Kuo & Taylor, 2004).

Living plants are also promoted as being therapeutic in learning environments. In 2018 researchers McCullough et al. (2018) described a "green wall" as an internal vertical garden which includes a growing medium of water and plants. These authors reported a link between the presence of green walls to minimise directed attention-fatigue and an increase in critical thinking. Previously, Van den Berg et al. (2016) had concluded from a controlled study of 170 children that green walls and living plants can provide a restorative design within primary classrooms. These approaches to supporting emotional wellbeing in a predictably stressful setting, such as a hospital waiting area or a learning setting of a school classroom, are invaluable.

The use of colour, and the height of ceilings and walls, was investigated in 1999 by Read et al. (1999). The findings indicated that play spaces in which the ceiling and walls were differentiated through height *or* colour supported demonstration of cooperative behaviour in pre-school children. Alternatively, undifferentiated space appeared to under-stimulate play, and reduce opportunities for cooperation between children.

Wardle (2018) recommends the use of specific colours in relation to expected outcomes, for example:

- Strong colours such as red and yellow to support development of gross motor skills.
- Subdued colours such as green and blue to support development of fine motor skills.
- White and lighter shades of colour to support activities which require directed attention.
- Pastel shades of colour to support activities which require involuntary attention.

This guidance is informative and presents a base of knowledge for discussion with a team of practitioners, and parents; however, each child's reaction and needs within a learning environment should be identified, and responded to, in the context of an organisational and community culture.

Some establishments refer to the Environmental Rating Scale (Harms & Clifford, 1998) in order to assess, evaluate, and develop the early years setting. This scale is representative of early years principles and curricula throughout the world, and includes categories of space and furnishings, personal care routines, language reasoning, activities, interaction, programme structure, and parents and staff, in addition to themes of literacy, mathematics, science and environment, and diversity.

Ultimately, inclusion of all children within mainstream services requires consideration of individual needs, wants, and interests which includes levels of sound, intensity of light, proprioception, emotional resilience to adversity, and ability to cope with planned or spontaneous changes in the structural or social environment. Needs will change as the child matures and necessitates a change in the environment. The creation of an inclusive learning environment is achievable through sharing of knowledge between parents, practitioners, and children, and understanding each child's interpretation and reaction to the proximal and distal world. The rationale of an early years environment should underpin the presentation of learning opportunities and focus upon ability, and attainment, as opposed to disability or perceived inability.

References

Barton, J. & Pretty, J. 2010, 'What is the best dose of nature and green exercise for improving mental health? A multi-study analysis', *Environmental Science and Technology*, vol. 44, no. 10, pp. 394–55. viewed 1 July, 2019, https://nhs.scot.knowledge.network.

Bernier, A., Carlson, S., Deschenes, M. & Matte-Gagne, C. 2012, 'Social factors in the development of early executive functioning: a closer look at the caregiving environment', viewed 1 January, 2012, https://ncbi.nlm.nih.gov/pubmed/222512882012.

Champagne, F.A. 2015, 'Epigenetics of the developing brain', *Zero to Three, Connecting Science, Policy, and Practice*, vol. 35, no. 3, pp. 2–8. Zero to Three, Washington.

Collado, S. & Staats, H. 2016, 'Contact with nature and children's restorative experiences: an eye to the future', *Journal of Frontiers in Psychology*, vol. 7. viewed 7 July 2019. DOI: 10.3389/fpsyg.2016.01885.

Corraliza, J.A., Collado, S. & Bethelmy, L. 2012, 'Nature as a moderator of stress in urban children', *Social and Behavioural Sciences*, vol. 38, pp. 253–63. viewed 20 July, 2019, https:sciencedirect.com/science/article/pii/S1877042812008269.

Furnivall, J. 2011, 'Attachment-informed practice with looked after children and young people', viewed 29 October, 2017, https://iriss.org.uk/resources/insights/attachment-informed-practice-looked-after.

Gailliot, M.T. & Baumeister, R.F. 2007, 'The physiology of willpower: linking blood glucose to self-control', *Personality and Social Psychology Review*, vol. 11, no. 4, pp. 303–27. DOI: 10.1177/1088868307303030S.

Gur, E. 2014, 'The effect of physical and environmental factors of a "child development centre" on a centre's selection', *International Journal of Architectural Research*. viewed 1 July, 2019, https://nhs.scot.knowledge.network.

Harms, T. & Clifford, R.M. 1998, *Early childhood environment rating scale*, Teachers College Press, New York.

Hunt, S., Virgo, S., Klett-Davies, M., Page, A. & Apps, J. 2011, 'Provider influence on the home learning environment', viewed 1 July 2011 from, http://education.gov.uk/publications/.

Ismail, F.Y., Fatemi, A. & Johnston, M.V. 2017, 'Cerebral plasticity: windows of opportunity in the developing brain', *European Journal of Paediatric Neurology*, vol. 21, no. 1, pp. 23–48. DOI: 10.1016/j.ejpn.2016.07.007.

Kaplan, S. 1995, 'The restorative benefits of nature: toward an integrative framework', *Journal of Environmental Psychology*, vol. 15, no. 3, pp. 169–82. viewed 1 July, 2019. https://nhs.scot.knowledge.network.

Kaplan, S. & Berman, M. 2010, 'Executive function and self-regulation', *Association for Psychological Science*, vol. 5, no. 1, pp. 43–57. viewed 18 July, 2019, https:www.sagepub.com/journalsPermissions.nav.

Kuo, F.E. & Taylor, A.F. 2004, 'A potential natural treatment for attention-deficit/hyperactivity disorder: evidence from a national study', *American Journal of Public Health*, vol. 94, no. 9, pp. 1580–6. viewed 1 July, 2019, https://www.ncbi.nlm.nih.gov/pubmed/153333182004

Louv, R. 2005, *Last child in the woods: saving our children from nature-deficit disorder*, Algonquin Books of Chapel Hill, New York.

McCullough, M.B., Martin, M.D. & Sajady, M.A. 2018, 'Implementing green walls in schools', *Frontiers in Psychology*, vol. 9, pp. 619. viewed 21 July, 2019. https ://www.frontiersin.org/articles/357834Psychol.

McLoyd, V.C. 1983, 'The effect of the structure of play objects on the pretend play of low income preschool children', *Society for Research in Child Development*, vol. 54, no. 3, pp. 626–35. viewed 5 July, 2019, https://www.jstor.org/stable/1 130049?seq=1.

Moore, T. 2015, *The developing genome: an introduction to behavioural epigenetics*, Oxford University Press, New York.

Moore, T., Arefadib, N., Deery, A. & West, S. 2017, 'The first thousand days: an evidence paper', viewed 30 September, 2017, www.rch.org.au/cch.

Moran, P., Ghate, D. & van der Merwe, A. 2004, *What works in parenting support? A review of the international evidence*, Department for Education and Skills, London.

Nitecki, E. & Chung, M. 2016, 'Play as place: a safe space for young children to learn about the world', *International Journal of Early Childhood Environmental Education*, vol. 4, pp. 1. viewed 1 July, 2019, https://eric.ed.gov/?id=EJ1120144.

O'Brien, L. & Murray, R. 2007, 'Forest school and its impact upon young children: case studies in Britain', viewed 28 March, 2018, www.forestresearch.gov.uk.

Ohly, H., White, M., Wheeler, B., Bethel, A., Ukoumunne, O., Nikolaou, V. & Garside, R. 2016, 'Attention restoration theory: a systematic review of the attention restoration potential of exposure to natural environments', *Journal of Toxicology and Environmental Health. Part B, Critical Reviews*, vol. 19, no. 7, pp. 7. DOI: 10.1080/10937404.2016.1196155.

Pote, I., Doubell, L., Brims, L., Larbie, J., Stock, L. & Lewing, B. 2019, 'Engaging disadvantaged and vulnerable parents, an evidence review', viewed 21 July, 2019, https://www.eif.org.uk/reports/engaging-disadvantaged-and-vulnerable-parents-an-evidence-review.

Read, M.A., Sugawara, A.I. & Brandt, J.A. 1999, 'The impact of space and colour in the physical environment on pre-school children's cooperative behaviour', *Environment and Behaviour*, vol. 31, no. 3, pp. 413–28. DOI: 10.1177/00139169921972173.

Robinson, C. & Brown, A.M. 2016, 'Considering sensory processing issues in trauma affected children: the physical environment in children's residential homes', *Scottish Journal of Residential Childcare*, vol. 15, pp. 1. viewed 1 January, 2019, https://nhs.scot.knowledge.network.

Royal College of Paediatrics & Child Health (RCPCH). 2019, 'State of child health, Scotland - Two years on', viewed 1 July, 2019, www.rcpch.ac.uk/state-of-child-health.

Scottish Government. 2018, 'Nurture, adverse childhood experiences and trauma informed practice: making the links between these approaches', viewed 1 January, 2019, https://nhs.scot.knowledge.network.

Simpson, S. 2009, 'Environmental checklist for autistic spectrum conditions (Part 2)', viewed 6 July, 2019, http://jessicasimpson.ws/environmental-checklist-for-autism-spectrum-conditions-part-2.html.

Van den Berg, A.E., Wesselius, J.E., Maas, J. & Tanja-Dijkstra, K. 2016, 'Green walls for a restorative classroom environment: a controlled evaluation study', *Environment and Behaviour*, vol. 49, no. 7, pp. 791–813. DOI: 10.1177/0013916516667976.

Wardle, F. 2018, 'Creating indoor environments for young children', *Early Childhood News*. viewed 4 November, 2018, http://earlychildhoodnews.com/earlychildhood/article_view.aspx?ArticleID=294.

Wilson, R. 1997, 'A sense of place', *Early Childhood Education Journal*, vol. 24, no. 3, pp. 3. viewed 5 July, 2019, https://nhs.scot.knowledge.network.

Winnicott, D.W. 1971, *Playing & Reality*, Tavistock Publications, London.

Zarra-Nezhad, M., Kiuru, N., Aunola, K., Zarra-Nezhad, M., Ahonen, T., Poikkeus, A., Lerkkanen, M. & Nurmi, J. 2014, 'Social withdrawal in children moderates the association between parenting styles and the children's own socioemotional development', *Journal of Child Psychology and Psychiatry, and Allied Disciplines*, vol. 55, no. 11, pp. 1260–9. DOI:10.1111/jcpp.12251.s.

4 Adverse childhood experiences, attachment, and the early years learning environment

The final chapter reviews the three concepts of adverse childhood experiences, attachment, and the early years learning environment. Links between the three topics which support a child's development and achievement of potential are discussed in a context of research and inclusive pedagogy.

There is a general understanding across disciplines that a learning environment has three integral components: the learner, the context, and the subject-matter (Blumenfeld et al., 2006). Over the past century, children's development in services has been supported by several different approaches, such as didactic teaching, supported exploration, or self-directed active learning. Active learning is the current philosophy which underpins implementation of early years curricula in many countries, and the theory relates to the constructivist model. An expected outcome was described by Bereiter and Scardamalia (1989) as children developing as *intentional* or *adaptive* learners. Similar concepts underpin curricula: for example, Scotland's Curriculum for Excellence is founded on the four outcomes of successful learners, confident individuals, responsible citizens, and effective contributors (Scottish Executive, 2004).

Goals and outcomes

Professionals and organisations are accountable, and implementation of service needs to be auditable. A consequence is that outcomes or goals, and an assessment process, need to be clearly identified and recorded for inspectorate and associated procedures. The terms "outcomes" and "goals" tend to be applied interchangeably in literature, but it is generally accepted that goals relate to a self-determined end product or acquired skill, and outcomes are relevant to developmental norms of childhood.

Cottle and Alexander (2013) conducted an investigation of "quality" in early years settings from the perspectives of the United Kingdom's Government, researchers, and practitioners. The findings indicated that government policies underpin the understanding of quality but implementation of the service is also affected by the local context of each setting.

Inspection is essential to maintain an accepted standard of care and education within each service, and throughout each nation. Standards tend to be set in a rationale of children achieving pre-determined outcomes, and these outcomes are based upon developmental norms; however, in recent years recognition has been given to the context which includes the needs of service-users. Inclusion for all children within mainstream services has caused researchers and educators to review, and to debate, whether the use of developmental norms is the best measure of a child's involvement and wellbeing within the learning environment. These norms align age with expected stage of development, and may not be met if a child has complex needs. Increasingly, emphasis is placed upon each child being supported through a responsive environment, secure attachment, and minimisation of the impact of adversities in order to achieve *his* or *her* potential.

Professionals and parents unite in supporting children in achieving potential (Whitters, 2019). Implications of potential include self-worth, achievement of one's own goals, and contribution to others. The question of how potential is assessed for an individual, and within the context of service-delivery, and evaluation, requires consideration and agreement by the child, parents, and professionals.

Involvement and wellbeing

The three concepts of childhood experiences, attachment, and the early years learning environment are complimentary and integral aspects to a child's uptake of knowledge, understanding, and attainment. It is important that the structural environment is not studied in isolation. As previously mentioned in Chapter 3, the physical structure of a learning space, and the artefacts within, may provide stimulating opportunities, and adhere to guidelines, but it is worth considering that activation of learning is dependent on influences from outside and inside the learner.

Some services use the Leuven Involvement and Wellbeing Scale by Laevers (1994) to gauge the child's engagement and emotional reaction to the learning environment. I have found this scale to be informative, and a source to gain insight into the child's learning capacity and ability. Wellbeing, and involvement with activities, are graded from one to five as separate entities during observations. Recording the scales at the beginning, middle, and conclusion of a short observation, for example over half an hour, provides information on entry transition, acclimatisation to a learning environment, executive functioning, and the exit transition. Deep insight is gained by consideration of similarities and differences between the two scales.

74 *Adversities, attachment, and environment*

The disparities can be informative, and occur despite the stimulating environment. Clarification is gained on the complexity of learning. For example, a child may have a high level of emotional wellbeing but a lower level of involvement with learning. Explanations could focus upon physiological needs such as fatigue, hunger, or thirst, or upon the child's personality. The child may desire to verbally interact with the adult/peers as opposed to engaging with activities, the artefacts may not relate to the child's specific interests, or he may wish to return to play with his peers elsewhere.

Alternatively, the child may have a low level of emotional wellbeing but demonstrate a high level of involvement. I have often observed children who are known to have experienced trauma, for example in a child protection context, compartmentalising their play from emotions. A child may turn his back to the play area and people, and operate at a high level of involvement upon an activity by himself but express a low level of emotional wellbeing within a relationship. This response can be regarded as a coping strategy by a child who is suffering from the impact of adversity. The child appears to minimise emotional impact upon his play experience, and this can only be achieved during solitary play.

Analysis of the Leuven Scale (Laevers, 1994) supports comprehension of the theory and practice of the core concepts which are associated with executive functioning: working memory, response inhibition, and task-shifting. Garon et al. (2008) described these concepts as separate but inter-connected.

The following aspects relate to interpretation of the five stages from the Leuven Scale (Laevers, 1994) within a practice context of early years, as quoted from my previous work (Whitters, 2018).

Child involvement

1. The child may observe the environment without involvement or create a barrier between himself and the setting, for example by covering his eyes or turning towards the carer.
2. The child's involvement at a basic sensory level is easily interrupted by an external factor which stops his interaction. The child may subsequently transfer his attention to a different activity, and commence interaction at the same basic sensory level.
3. The child's involvement does not have a focus. He is easily distracted by internal or external influences but can resume interaction with the same activity at a sensory level.
4. The child appears to have a plan and focus for involvement in play. He is able to concentrate on the activity for short periods by filtering out potential distractions.

5. Fully engaged in meaningful play – the child demonstrates that he is following his interests, creating, and implementing a plan, and responding to his needs by accessing support as required. The child demonstrates a deep level of learning through the use of three stages – sensory exploration; implementation of knowledge and of understanding from implicit or explicit memories; and extrapolating by using his imagination and quest for knowledge.

Child wellbeing

1. The child shows clear signals of distress and may attempt to leave the environment or to seek support from the carer. The child demonstrates rejection of the learning opportunities by his physical and emotional responses.
2. The child may observe but not interact with the environment. Facial expression and neutral posture show little or no emotion, and he will keep his body still.
3. Facial expression and posture demonstrate that the child is beginning to relax and feels comfortable enough to interact within the environment. The child may stand and play in one area.
4. The child demonstrates obvious signs of self-confidence and enjoyment in play. His increasing sense of self will be demonstrated by an increase in physical movement throughout the learning environment.
5. The child demonstrates obvious signs of self-confidence and high self-esteem. His body language expresses a high level of wellbeing by the use of physical skills to increase interaction with the environment.

Bereiter and Scardamalia (1989) reviewed the processes of traditional teaching and self-directed instruction, and posed interesting points regarding the constitution of intentional learning described as the cognitive processes which support the ultimate goal of learning. These researchers raised issues which are still relevant 30 years later. An example for reflection which can be constructed from this research is: "Can intentional involvement with the learning environment only occur if it is observable by another person?"

It seems that this status of intentional involvement would require a practitioner:

- To observe a child during experiential play.
- To accurately predict the child's intended goal.
- To assess if the child is participating in processes associated with the goal.
- To decide if the child has achieved his goal.

Research by Walsh and Gardner (2005) highlights failure as implicit in the delivery of a curriculum with formal prescribed outcomes, and present the play-based curriculum as an alternative approach. Key features of this example of active learning through experience are described by these researchers as **internal** to the child and focus upon emotion, resilience, and subsequently an increase in involvement with the environment. Descriptors of this self-directed learning include the child feeling secure, being engaged, using meta-cognitive skills, and demonstrating social skills in interaction with peers. Emotional wellbeing is intrinsic to learning and development, with an outcome of the child being an active agent, and developing a sense of the autobiographical self.

An understanding of self has five stages: physical agent, social agent, teleological agent, intentional mental agent, and autobiographical self (Trevarthan & Aitken, 2001). Achievement of these inter-dependent stages of human development tends to occur sequentially but children who have experienced trauma may have gaps in development, and an immature understanding of self which directly affects interpretation and interaction with the world. Miell (1995) found that the average child will gain baseline comprehension of the autobiographical self at approximately five years of age.

Blumenfeld et al. (2006) also reviewed the theory of learning environments, and identified similar sub-sets relating to aspects within the child: motivation, communication, cognitive thinking and reasoning, and self-regulated learning. The research described influential factors to learning as developmental stage, accuracy of language, culture and context, adaptation, design and build of learning environment, community of practice, scaling-up and transferring knowledge, educator's skills, and finally diversity. Many of these issues have informed the creation of curricula, and they are presented within principles and practice guidance, for example the Common Assessment Framework in England (Department for Children, Schools and Families, 2009). The commonality between research and today's practice in early years is the promotion of a child's motivation to seek out, to identify, and to embrace learning opportunities.

Greater comprehension of the impact of adversity in the context of early childhood has clarified aspects of brain development in the pre-birth period, and the unique interpretation and reaction to experiences by each human being. Research on internal influences has given the field an understanding of the impact of relationships, and links to a child's ability and capacity to learn. It is widely accepted that a secure attachment relationship in the early years supports a child in participating in active learning, in demonstrating motivation to problem-solve, and in gaining resilience to short- and long-term adversities. The inner working model of a child is continuously updated, and directs his reaction and interaction to external experiences. Neuroscience has given the early years field deep insight into brain development and influences from the external world, in addition to the significance of the first 1,000 days of learning post-birth.

Knowledge creation

In a later work by Bereiter and Scardamalia (2014), significance is placed upon "students" or learners, taking joint ownership with educators for their uptake of knowledge and ultimately an increase in understanding. Knowledge creation, as termed by these authors, is presented as a cultural practice with relevance to the context. This study highlights the challenge for educators in creating a responsive environment which contributes to knowledge building for each child, and promotes positivity in childhood.

Community of practice

Evolvement of a **community of practice** was presented by Lave and Wenger (1991) who described the emergence of culture in organisations and communities. Early years services are immersed in a local culture as most families will live in the area. Services which have a larger catchment area are still influenced by the community in which the organisation is based due to the use of natural outdoor areas, and promotion of leisure facilities, for example, sports halls, swimming pools, and libraries. The rationale in the use of extended environments, beyond the early years structural building, is to present a broad education and life skills to the developing child.

The layout of a learning environment can encourage or inhibit the development of a community of practice. Universal features can be adapted, for example, children's choices, multiple types of spaces for playing individually or in pairs and larger groups, and representation of diversity which reflects and responds to needs. Also, the structural environment, and ethos, should celebrate different abilities and skills as integral to the group and setting. An inclusive pedagogy embraces lifestyles and respects religious beliefs.

Over time, children and adults will internalise the culture of an establishment, and this absorption of the socio–cultural knowledge of a learning environment increases opportunities to participate. Lave and Wenger (1991) express that the existence of a community of practice is essential to acquisition of knowledge through the sharing of meaning. A major source of learning, and promotion of meaning in an early years setting, is role-modelling by adults and peers which leads to copying and developing skills based upon an increase in understanding.

Schemas

Every early years care and education student will learn about schemas on an undergraduate course. The basic level of comprehension of this concept is the child's use of patterns of play which allow him or her to explore interests and to interpret the world in relation to him or herself. Over time these patterns have been formalised and placed within categories which describe the repetitive element of the child's actions.

Example of schemas:

- Trajectory – reaching and stretching up, down, and across for objects using hands and feet.
- Rotation – spinning self or objects, rolling, and tumbling, with or without equipment.
- Enclosing – creating boundaries with pens on paper, or artefacts, like bricks.
- Enveloping – dressing up, hiding and emerging, wrapping items, and making dens.
- Transporting – a theme of moving from one place to another, whether objects or self.
- Connecting – fastening objects together with complicated plans and determination.
- Positioning – arranging and sorting repeatedly with similar order.
- Orientation – exploring the world from different heights and angles.

(Education Scotland, 2019)

Curricular guidance emphasises the importance of key workers acknowledging the child's fluctuating interests as expressed by schemas, and providing stimulating opportunities which respond to, and encourage, these concepts in practice (Louis et al., 2018). The rationale is that the construction of knowledge and understanding through schemas supports consolidation of learning and potential for applicability to many environments and circumstances.

Example from practice

Helena has three children, two school-girls and a two-and-a-half-year-old son called Nikodem. Today, the lunch dishes had been washed and left to drip-dry, the washing machine was spinning noisily on the last cycle, it was an hour before the school-run, and Helena was sitting down... just for a few minutes.

Nikodem had taken control of the living-room space, and he had spread multiple toy vehicles and two garages across the navy blue carpet, and under the low wooden table. As Helena glanced at her son's activities, she was reminded of an article in the monthly nursery newsletter, sectioned "Parents' Tips on Play." A few moments later and Helena had recovered the coloured paper from the recycling bin. She unfolded it carefully, and smoothed out the pages with anticipation.

The topic was introduced as **Schemas**, and depicted cartoon characters playing in different ways with arrows which led Helena to a list of play categories. The topic was described as an important play stage which provided children with meaning and understanding of the world. The mother's interest was captured, and her fair hair swung forward as she bent her head over the leaflet. Nikodem was distracted for a few seconds by this movement in the periphery of his learning arena, but the presence of his attachment figure represented the circle of security, and the little boy quickly returned to moving a white and red ambulance between the table-legs. Nikodem was sitting on the carpet on top of his feet as little children often do. Feet were crossed, back straight, two hands free for exploring – a good balancing position for Nikodem to stretch for his favourite vehicles, and a good starting block to rapidly rise onto his knees and begin an upright crawl across the carpet to the green garage.

Helena looked up from the cartoon characters on the newsletter towards Nikodem, and she decided that the categories of transporting and positioning toys were easily applicable to her son's play. For a few significant moments this young mum took time to notice her little boy's play, to reflect and to understand his intricate planning and careful execution in patterns of movement as he traversed the play space, and to feel pride in his achievement.

Marshall and Lewis (2013) identified the importance of environmental influences on speech and communication skills in young children. This study reported that speech and language delay occurs in approximately 6% of the child population within the United Kingdom. An awareness of schemas by parents and practitioners leads to an increase in provision of the opportunities to extend a child's vocabulary. The use of adjectives, prepositions, and verbs during the play sessions support neural networks to link concepts, and ultimately language.

Schemas should be welcomed and supported by choices of artefacts which expose children to the schema of interest but also to other schemas. Children can be encouraged to extend their play by the introduction of multiple schemas through perceptive scaffolding by an adult, and sensitive responding in the nursery or home environment. This stage of play may be short- or long-term, and each child will demonstrate determination in reproducing patterns, achieving own goals, and making meaning within his or her chosen play context. An increase in knowledge and understanding is transferrable, and key workers can record the achievement within the child's file, and share with the parent or carer.

Conclusion

Children need to be offered a wide variety of learning opportunities but most importantly play must occur in the actual presence, or working memory, of a secure attachment figure. This circle of security, existing initially in practice as a baby in a parent's arms, or latterly through recourse to implicit memory, is the catalyst which supports our youngest citizens to seek out learning, to minimise the effect of adversities, to increase executive functioning, and to enjoy a fulfilling childhood.

References

Bereiter, C. & Scardamalia, M. 1989, 'Intentional learning as a goal of instruction', in L.B. Resnick (ed.), *Knowing, learning and instruction: essays in honour of Robert Glaser*, Erlbaum, Hillsdale, pp. 361–92.

Bereiter, C. & Scardamalia, M. 2014, 'Knowledge building and knowledge creation: one concept, two hills to climb', in S.C. Tan, H.J. So & J. Yeo (eds.), *Knowledge creation in education*, Springer, Singapore, pp. 35–52.

Blumenfeld, P.C., Marx, R.W. & Harris, C. 2006, 'Learning environments', in W. Damon & R.M. Lerner (eds.), *Handbook of child psychology*, vol. 4, Wiley & Sons, New Jersey, pp. 297–342.

Cottle, M. & Alexander, E. 2013, 'Quality in early years settings: government research and practitioners' perspectives', *British Educational Research Journal*. DOI:10.1080/01411926.2011.571661.

Department for Children, Schools and Families. 2009, Common assessment framework. viewed March 11, 2009, http://dcsf.gov.uk/everychildmatters/strategy/deliveringservices1/caf/cafframework.

Education Scotland. 2019. 'Schematic play', February 27, viewed 26 July, 2019, https://education.gov.scot/improvement/learning-resources/schematic-play.

Garon, N., Bryson, S.E. & Smith, I.M. 2008, 'Executive function in pre-schoolers: a review using an integrative framework', *Psychological Bulletin*, vol. 134, pp. 1. viewed 7 December, 2017, www.nhs.scot.knowledge.network.

Laevers, F. 1994, *Defining and assessing quality in early childhood education*, Studia Pedagogica: Leuven University Press.

Lave, J. & Wenger, E. 1991, *Situated learning, legitimate peripheral participation*, Cambridge University Press, New York, 29–55.

Louis, S., Beswick, C. & Featherstone, S. 2018, *Understanding schemas in young children: again! again!* Featherstone Professional Development, London.

Marshall, J. & Lewis, E. 2013, "It's the way you talk to them.' The child's environment: early years practitioners' perceptions of its influence on speech and language development, its assessment and environment targeted interventions',*Child Language, Teaching and Therapy*, vol. 30, no. 3, pp. 337–52. DOI: 10.1177/0265590113516331.

Miell, D. 1995, 'The development of self', in P. Barnes (ed.), *Personal, social and emotional development of children*, Open University, Blackwell, pp. 190–201.

Scottish Executive. 2004, *The curriculum for excellence*, Scottish Executive, Edinburgh.

Trevarthan, C. & Aitken, K.J. 2001, 'Infant intersubjectivity: research, theory, and clinical applications', *Journal of Child Psychology and Psychiatry, and Allied Disciplines,* vol. 42, Cambridge University Press, Cambridge.

Walsh, G. & Gardner, J. 2005, Assessing the quality of early years learning environments. *Early Childhood Research and Practice*, vol. 7, pp. 1. viewed 23 July, 2019, http://ecrp.uiuc.edu/v7n1/walsh.html.

Whitters, H.G. 2018, *Family learning to inclusion in the early years: theory, practice and partnerships*, Routledge, Abingdon, pp. 52–4.

Whitters, H.G. 2019, *Attainment and executive functioning in the early years: research for inclusive practice and lifelong learning*, Routledge, Abingdon, pp. 7.

Index

abuse 7, 12, 14, 17, 43
active learning 72, 76
adaptation 49, 56
adverse childhood experiences (ACEs): abuse 7, 12, 14, 17, 43; attachment and 34–35, 42–43; brain development and 76; cognition and 10; complex trauma and 42–44; deficit model of 6, 10; early intervention for 18–23; epigenetics and 11; extrinsic feedback and 17; household adversities and 7; intergenerational effect of 16–17, 37–38, 50–51; interventions for 7; mental health and 9, 64; neglect and 7, 14, 43; post-traumatic stress disorder (PTSD) and 11–12; poverty and 8, 51, 64; pre-verbal stage and 57; research on 2–3, 7–17; resilience and 16–18; stress hormones and 15; suicide risk and 11; toxic stress and 8, 42, 49, 51; trauma-informed practice 10–11; types of 7
affect regulation 43
Ahonen, T. 51
Ainsworth, M. 28, 34
Alexander, E. 72
Alford, S. M. 10
Allen, G. 12
Almeida, T. 10
Anda, R. 10
Anda, R. F. 3, 7, 8, 10
approach motivation 13, 17
Arefadib, N. 49, 51

attachment: behavioural control and 42–43; biological processes and 38; circle of security and 28, 36; defining 29; development of theory 28; environment and 40–41; influence on future relationships 34; insecure 29, 42; interventions for 41; learning and 40; nurturing and 40–41; positive relationships and 3; practitioners and 3–4, 28–29, 39–40; resilience and 5; secure 28–29, 39–41, 43; trauma-informed practice 43
attachment disorders 29
attachment figures: affirmation of achievement and 35; empathic responding and 39; influences of 36; learned helplessness and 13–14; learning and 27; miscuing by 38–39; positivity and 13; removing/minimising threats and 35; resilience and 44; sense of self and 23, 35; transitions in 57
attention deficit hyperactivity disorder (ADHD) 29, 66
attention restoration theory 4, 65–66
attribution 36
Aunola, K. 51
autistic spectrum disorders 29, 50, 58
avoidance motivation 13, 15, 17

Baban, A. 8
Barton, J. 62
Bearer, E. L. 11
Beckwith, H. 29

behaviour management 30–32, 37
Bellis, M. A. 8
Bereiter, C. 72, 75, 77
Berman, M. 66
Bernier, A. 51
Bethel, A. 65
Bethelmy, L. 67
Blumenfeld, P. C. 76
body language 31–32
Borge, A. I. 41
Bowlby, John: attachment theory and 3, 28, 33–35; biography 32–33; on inner working model 36; on maternal separation 30, 33–34
brain: chemical signals in 13, 15; development of 2, 12, 16, 77; environmental stress and 12; impact of adversity and 76; impact of stimulation on 12; memory and 13; plasticity of 5, 8, 12, 35, 50
Brandt, J. A. 68
Bretherton, I. 35–36
Bright, M. A. 10
Brown, A. M. 57
Bryson, S. E. 74

Cardoso, J. 10
Carlson, S. 51
child development: adverse childhood experiences (ACEs) and 7, 12; approach and avoidance motivation in 13, 17; approaches to 72; attachment and 3–4, 29; brain development and 2, 12, 16; exploratory influences 51; inner working model and 36; language development and 17; pre-verbal stage 57; resilience and 4, 14, 17; schemas and 78–80; secure attachment and 51; sense of self 23, 30, 76; speech and communication skills 79; transitions in 53–55
childhood aggression 36–37
children: executive functioning 8, 13, 17, 30, 37; home environments and 4; as intentional/adaptive learners 72; involvement in learning environment 73–76; psychiatric disorders and 29; self-directed learning and 76; services environments and 4; wellbeing and 73–75

Chung, M. 49
circle of security 28, 36
Circle of Security Project 38–39
cognition 10
Collado, S. 67
Common Assessment Framework (England) 76
community of practice 77
complex trauma 42–44
Cooper, G. 28
Corraliza, J. A. 67
Côté, S. M. 41
Cottle, M. 72
Coughlan, B. 29
cultural sensitivity 56
Curriculum for Excellence (Scotland) 72

Deery, A. 49, 51
Deschenes, M. 51
Devaney, J. 11
developmental plasticity 49
directed attention 66
disinhibited attachment disorders 29
dissociation 43–44
Duffy, M. 11
Duschinsky, R. 29

Early Intervention (Allen) 12
Eco-Schools programme 3, 8–9
Edwards, D. 12
Edwards, V. 3, 7, 8, 10
Elfer, P. 40
emotional wellbeing 74, 76
Environmental Rating Scale 68
environmental sensitivity 62
environmental stress 12
epigenetics 11, 50
European Child Maltreatment Prevention Action Plan 2015–2020 10
executive functioning: attachment and 40; glucose and 64; motivation to learn and 13; poverty and 8; promotion of positive behaviour and 30; reflection and 38; sense of self and 17; set-shifting and 37
explicit memory 32, 57

family adversities 49–50
family learning 20–22, 41
Felitti, V. J. 3, 7, 8, 10

Fernandez-Baca, D.E. 10
Fisher, P. 8
Fonagy, P. 37
Forest Schools 62
Forslund, T. 29
Foster, S. L. 29
foster care 57
Furnivall, J. 57

Galinsky, E. 38
Gardner, J. 76
Garon, N. 74
Garside, R. 65
genome 50
Geoffroy, M. C. 41
Getting It Right for Every Child (Scottish Government) 8
Ghate, D. 56
glucose 64
green exercise 58, 62
green spaces 4, 66; *see also* natural environment
green walls 4, 67
Gur, E. 58

hard fascination activities 65–66
Harris, C. 76
health: attention restoration theory and 65; childbirth and 12; interventions for 8, 10–11; natural environments and 62–64, 66; prenatal 49–50; resilience and 16; secure attachment and 38; social determinants for 51; *see also* mental health
Hinojosa, M. S. 10
Hoffman, K. 28
home environments 4, 7, 40, 53
household adversities 7
Howes, C. 38
Hughes, K. 8

imaginative play 22, 67
implicit memory 13, 32
indoor environments: arts and crafts/creative imaginative play 61; book corner and physical play 61–62; children's choice area 59–60; color in 67–68; floor play and table-top areas 61; learning in 58–59; natural environment and 67–68; snack and tooth-brushing area 60

inner working model 36
insecure attachment 29, 42
interactive play 20–23
interventions: attachment and 41; early 18–20; family learning 20–23; for health 8, 10–11; interactive play 20–23; trauma-informed approach to 23
involuntary attention 66
Iskakova, A. 41

Jones, L. 8

Kachaeva, M. 8
Kaplan, S. 65–66
Kiuru, N. 51
Knapp, C. 10
knowledge creation 77
Kontos, S. 38
Koss, M. P. 3, 7, 8, 10
Kuo, F. E. 66

Laevers, F. 73
language development 17
Larkin, H. 10
Larouche, F. 41
Lave, J. 77
learned helplessness 13–14
learning: active 72, 76; approach motivation and 13; attachment figures and 27; attention restoration theory and 65–66; intentional 72, 75; knowledge creation and 77; motivation for 13, 76; secure attachment and 40; self-directed 76
learning environments: adverse childhood experiences and 2; arts and crafts/creative imaginative play 61; attachment relationship and 1; book corner and physical play 61–62; child-led play in 48; children's choice area 59–60; choice of settings 58; communities of practice and 77; components of 72; cultural sensitivity in 56; developmental stages and 76; epigenetics and 50–51; floor play and table-top areas 61; genetics and 49–50; in the home 4, 53; indoor setting 58–62, 67–68; involvement in 73–76; outdoors 4, 62–67;

place-based education and 49; play structures in 66–67; positive behaviour and 55; relationship-based practice 42, 56, 58; residential care 57; services and 4; snack and tooth-brushing area 60; social determinants and 51; stress responses and 1; transitions in 53–55; wellbeing and 73–74
Leckenby, N. 8
Lerkkanen, M. 51
Leuven Involvement and Wellbeing Scale 73–74
Lewis, E. 79
Locke, J. 35
Louv, R. 62

Maas, J. 67
Marks, J. S. 3, 7, 8, 10
Marshall, J. 79
Martin, M. D. 67
Marvin, R. 28
Marx, R. W. 76
Matte-Gagne, C. 51
McCullough, M. B. 67
McLoyd, V. C. 66
mental health 4, 8–9, 33–34, 38, 62
mentalisation 37
Miell, D. 76
Moore, T. 49–51
Moran, P. 56
motivation: approach 12–13, 17; avoidance 12–13, 15, 17; extrinsic feedback and 17; intrinsic drivers for 17; learned helplessness and 13–14; learning and 13, 76; play and 23
Mulligan, B. S. 11
Munholland, K. A. 35–36
Murray, J. 41

National Child Traumatic Stress Network 42
National Council on Children, Families and Relationships 16
National Institute for Health and Care Excellence (NICE) 9
National Scientific Council on the Developing Child 12
natural environment: attention restoration theory and 65–66; directed attention and 66; health and 62–64, 66; indoor environments and 67–68; learning environments and 58, 62; play in 4, 67; therapeutic value of 67; *see also* outdoor environments
nature deficit disorder 62
negative behaviour 17–18, 31, 37
neglect 7, 14, 43
neuroplasticity 49
neuroscience 12–13, 35, 77
Nikolaou, V. 65
Nitecki, E. 49
non-genomic transmission of disease 50
Nordenberg, D. 3, 7, 8, 10
Nurmi, J. 51
nurturing 40–41

Ohly, H. 65
outdoor environments: attention deficit hyperactivity disorder (ADHD) and 66; attention restoration theory and 4, 65–66; environmental sensitivity and 62; green play areas in 58; health benefits of 62; involuntary attention and 66; play structures in 66–67; provision of 63–65; resilience and 16; services for 4; wellbeing and 64; *see also* natural environment
outdoor nurseries 62, 64

Page, J. 40
Pal, S. 29
Palfi, S. 41
parental resilience 16
parent-child relationships 16, 19, 22
parenting: couples interventions and 52; early interventions and 18–23, 41–42; empathic responding and 39; interactive 21–23; learned helplessness and 14; practitioners and 41–42, 52–53; resilience and 16; responsive 17–18; skills development 18–22; styles of 51; transition strategies 54–55; video interactive guidance (VIG) for 18, 21
parenting programmes 21, 23, 38, 56
Perry, B. 16
place-based education 49

play: child-led 48; color and 68; creative and imaginative 61; curiosity and 23; family learning and 20–21; floor and table-top 61; imaginative 22, 67; indoor settings for 61–62; interactive 20–23; outdoor 62–67; physical 61–62; positive 21; role modelling in 19–20; schemas and 78–80; social boundaries and 22; structural environments 66–67
Poikkeus, A. 51
positive behaviour 30–32, 55
Positive Parenting Programme (Triple P) 21
positive play 21, 30
post-traumatic stress disorder (PTSD) 11–12
poverty 3, 8, 51, 63–64
Povilaitis, R. 8
Powell, B. 28
Pretty, J. 62
pre-verbal stage 57
Public Health Wales NHS Trust 7
Pudule, I. 8

Qirjako, G. 8

Raleva, M. 8
Ramos, C. 10
reactive attachment disorders 29
Read, M. A. 68
Reducing Parent Conflict 41
reflection 38
relationship-based practice 7, 42, 56
residential care 57
resilience: adverse childhood experiences (ACEs) and 7, 16–18; attachment figures and 4, 39, 44; development of 4, 14, 17, 21; emotional 36, 68; learning and 5; mental health and 9; outdoor exercise and 16; parental 16; self-directed learning and 76; stress responses and 10; transitions and 5, 53
Robertson, J. 3, 28, 33
Robinson, C. 57
role modelling 19–20, 30–31, 37
Royal College of Paediatrics and Child Health 64
Rutter, M. 41

Sajady, M. A. 67
Scardamalia, M. 72, 75, 77
schemas 78–80
Schore, A. N. 38
Schuengel, C. 29
Scottish Government 8, 9, 63
Scottish Mental Health Strategy 2017–2027 9
Séguin, J. R. 41
self-regulation 31–32, 43, 64
sense of self 23, 30, 35, 76
sensory awareness 57
services: accountability in 41; assessment of 72–73; communities of practice and 77; goals/outcomes of 72–73; learning environments and 4; parent-practitioner relationships 41–42, 52–53; physical structures of 58; relationship-based practice 58; resilience and 16; secure attachment in 39–41; transitions in 57
Shonkoff, J. P. 8
Smith, I. M. 74
Smith, L. 7
social boundaries 22–23, 29–32
social determinants 51
soft fascination activities 66
Sousa, S. 10
speech and communication skills 79
Spitz, A. M. 3, 7, 8, 10
Staats, H. 67
stress: avoidance motivation and 15; emotional 49; environmental 12; lack of reciprocity and 38; post-traumatic 11–13, 43, 57; poverty and 8, 51; self-regulation and 39; tolerable 6, 15, 17, 23, 39; toxic 8, 23, 42, 49, 51; trauma-informed practice and 10, 40
Sugawara, A. I. 68
Sustainable Development Goals 9

Tajiyeva, M. 41
Tanja-Dijkstra, K. 67
Taylor, A. F. 66
Terzic, N. 8
Teszenyi, E. 41
tolerable stress 6, 15, 17, 23, 39
toxic stress 8, 23, 42, 49, 51
transitional phenomena 54

transitions 53–55, 57
trauma-informed practice 10–11, 23
Turner, M. 29

Ukoumunne, O. 65
Ulukol, B. 8
United Nations 9

Van den Berg, A. E. 67
Van der Kolk, B. 39
van der Merwe, A. 56
Varga, A. N. 41
video interactive guidance (VIG) 18, 21
voluntary attention 66

Walsh, G. 76
Wardle, F. 68
wellbeing 64, 73–76
Wenger, E. 77
Wesselius, J. E. 67
West, S. 49, 51
Wheeler, B. 65
White, M. 65
Williamson, D. F. 3, 7, 8, 10
Wilson, R. 62
Winnicott, D. W. 54
World Health Organisation 10, 16, 34

Zarra-Nezhad, M. 51

For Product Safety Concerns and Information please contact our EU representative GPSR@taylorandfrancis.com
Taylor & Francis Verlag GmbH, Kaufingerstraße 24, 80331 München, Germany

www.ingramcontent.com/pod-product-compliance
Lightning Source LLC
Chambersburg PA
CBHW051759230426
43670CB00012B/2352